MASTERCLASS

Brazilian Jiu Jitsu

THE ULTIMATE GUARD

by
Gerson Sanginitto

EMPIRE Books
P.O. Box 431788, Los Angeles, CA 90049

I0370746

Disclaimer
Please note that the author and publisher of this book are NOT RESPONSIBLE in any manner whatsoever for any injury that may result from practicing the techniques and/or following the instructions given within. Since the physical activities described herein may be too strenuous in nature for some readers to engage in safely, it is essential that a physician be consulted prior to training.

Published in 2006 by Empire Books.
Copyright © 2006 by Empire Books.

All rights reserved. No part of this publication may be reproduced or utilized in any form or by any means, electronic or mechanical, including photocopying, recording, or by any information storage and retrieval system, without prior written permission from Empire Books.

Library of Congress Cataloging-in-Publication Data

ISBN-10: 1-933901-08-X
ISBN-13: 978-1-933901-08-4

Sanginitto, Gerson, 1965-
  Masterclass Brazilian jiu jitsu : the ultimate guard / by Gerson Sanginitto. -- 1st ed.
      p. cm.
  Includes index.
  ISBN 1-933901-08-X (pbk. : alk. paper)
 1. Jiu-jitsu--Brazil. I. Title. II. Title: Brazilian jiu jitsu. III. Title: Jiu jitsu.
  GV1114.S274 2006
  796.815'2--dc22
                                    2006009376
Empire Books
P.O. Box 491788
Los Angeles, CA 90049
(818) 767-7900

First edition
07 06 05 04 03 02 01 00 99 98 97 1 3 5 7 9 10 8 6 4 2
Printed in the United States of America.

Editor: David Tadman
Action Photography: Tom Fitzpatrick
Interior Photography: Jason Alan
Interior & Cover Design: Mario M. Rodriguez, MMR Design Solutions

This book is dedicated to Carina Sanginitto for her untiring dedication and support to all my projects, and for being the best wife in the world.

ACKNOWLEDGEMENT

To David Tadman, editor of the work, for his time and effort cleaning and polishing the manuscript. Your help and dedication is truly appreciated.

To Jason Alan, our photographer, who put in many hours in front of the camera capturing all the technical details.

To Jeremy Geaga, who provided excellent cooperation and skills while demonstrating the techniques in this book.

To Tom Fitzpatrick, who supplied wonderful action and competition photographs to also illustrate the book.

To Carlos Gracie Jr., president of the Brazilian Confederation of Jiu Jitsu, for his support throughout the years.

GERSON SANGINITTO

Gerson Sanginitto is one of the most well-known and respected Jiu-Jitsu teachers in the United States. Being a champion in Brazil where he began training in Judo, Gerson competed against the biggest names in the sport. With countless matches in the top tournaments and having gained great experience within the sport, Sanginitto is very familiar with the many techniques that work on the mat. But more than that, he is familiar with how life works with and without the art of Jiu-Jitsu. Gerson has more than paid his dues in becoming a successful martial arts instructor and mentor. What sets Gerson Sanginitto apart is an uncanny ability to relate to and understand people from all walks of life. Gerson Sanginitto's striving for excellence does not keep him in one place for long. "If you're not moving forward he says, then you're going backwards. I always try to challenge myself with new ideas and projects." With his commitment to expand Jiu-Jitsu in the United States and using the art to help students better themselves both physically and mentally, Sanginitto is at the forefront of the modern Jiu-Jitsu and grappling movement. His many years of training and experience have allowed him to internalize the important aspects of Jiu-Jitsu. Be it moral or the technical aspects of Jiu-Jitsu, he uses what he's learned in his life's daily routine. His knowledge and understanding of the technical aspects of Judo make him one of the best coaches in America and brings much hope to grappling practitioners and fans everywhere when he says, "The best is yet to come for Brazilian Jiu Jitsu in the United States."

TABLE OF CONTENTS

Introduction   viii

The Close Guard   1

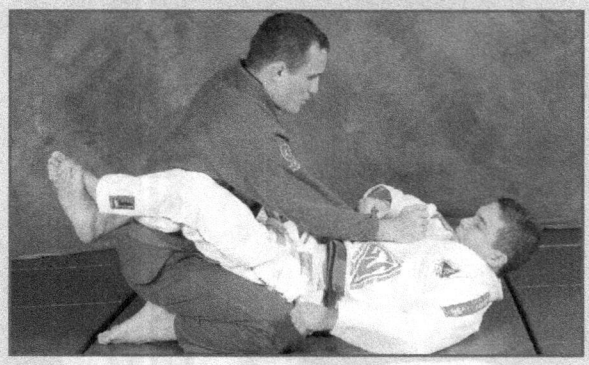

The Open Guard   82

The Half Guard 162

The Spider Guard 180

Conclusion 198

PREFACE

It is my hope that it would be understood, I do not hold claim to, or suggest that, the origins of the subject matter that lay within this book were originally conceived by the Author himself. It is the goal of the Author to teach what was been taught to him from past years, while at the same time bringing a new perspective on the subject matter to the masses. It is my goal to highlight within this book, the guard technique that is used in Brazilian Jiu Jitsu. You will find that this book gives sound knowledge of the subject matter at hand, covering the fundamentals and techniques being used, while at the same time showing visually, the outstanding examples that are captured inside.

This is not a book of Jiu Jitsu miracles, nor will you find any deep routed secrets within. That is for the simple reason there are no such miracles and secrets in Brazilian Jiu Jitsu. Brazilian Jiu Jitsu is nothing more than a proven art and science and requires nothing more than correct and proper practice and guidance. In short, this book will teach you all that is needed to learn about the specifics and essential aspects of the guard.

I have made the attempt to insure that you will hopefully master the mechanics of Brazilian Jiu Jitsu, but technique unfortunately, or fortunately, can only be learned through physical training and the proper supervision of an expert instructor. Thus brings us to the questions of how you, the student, can make full use of this book. For one, you must have a partner so that both of you can watch each other while practicing, to prevent any unwarranted injuries. Any practice, if uncontrolled, can be very dangerous.

You must learn these movements thoroughly. Study them all carefully in detail. One can never know too much technique. Above all, one must train hard in and out of the school. Conscientiously, seriously and courageously should be the creed to follow.

The Author

INTRODUCTION

To generalize Brazilian Jiu Jitsu as a gentle art in which strength is not required, one simply needs to use their opponent's strength as mental and physical balance, can be very misleading if taken too literally. While it is true that the main concept of Jiu Jitsu is "giving way to strength," it is equally true that the stronger man, given equal skill, will usually win in a Brazilian Jiu Jitsu match. Strength of course is needed, but more importantly, it is the understanding of how to use it. The main idea is to resist your opponent's strength by applying your own in the direct on in which he is weakest and unlikely to defend against it. In order to do this, the Brazilian Jiu Jitsu practitioner will need to have a certain amount of control of his opponent's position and movements. It is here where the use of the guard comes into play.

When the Brazilian Jiu Jitsu fighter uses the guard it is important to remember that all motion in the art of Jiu Jitsu is continuous, one movement merging undetectably into the next without break or pause. For the purposes of instruction, it is necessary to break down the continuous movements into the divers legs, arms and body movements, which cover the whole movements. The student should visualize a particular technique holistically and not as a series of separate movements that somehow are linked together. For the purposes of the book, the movements are described to one side only, but the student should practice using both sides, understanding the "left for right" and "right for left" when practicing to the opposite of your training partner.

Photo by Holly Stein

Introduction

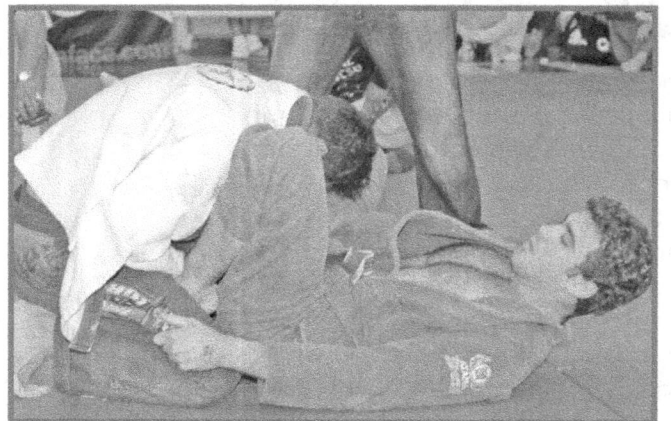

As the student progresses in the art, he will begin to see how quick changes and adjustments in the body position can wrest success from failure. The student will learn to combine chokes with arm-locks along with sweeps with reversals, using one as a feint to persuade his opponent to leave himself open. These are all important points which can be better leaned from experience and intelligent observation, than from studying the pages of a book.

In November 1993, Royce Gracie won the first Ultimate Fighting Championship easily, by controlling bigger opponents by fighting on his back and wrapping his legs around the body of his adversary. This technique is called "the guard" in Brazilian Jiu Jitsu. Months later after that first UFC Championship, exponents of many and diverse styles of martial arts were using this technique to explain their own style's system in fighting on the ground.

Neither Royce Gracie nor his father, the great Helio Gracie invented the "guard," but the fact remains it was Helio Gracie who tested and developed it to the point where it became the essential technical element for a small man to control a bigger opponent. The "guard" is the heart of good Brazilian Jiu Jitsu. No fighter/competitor will progress very far in the art without mastering it.

The fundamentals of the "close guard," in Brazilian Jiu Jitsu have evolved and brought forth many other modifications like; the open guard, the spider guard, the butterfly guard and the half-guard. All these have become a matter of serious study. They are highly necessary if the Brazilian Jiu Jitsu fighter wants to succeed in sport competition. The combinations and variations of the basic moves create a tapestry of technical difficulty that can only be read with a deep knowledge and understanding by one whom immerses himself within the proper training.

In all aspects of the different "guard positions" certain points should be carefully observed:

1. The whole body must always be comfortably relaxed.
2. The weight of the attacker's body should be on the mat and not on you.
3. Once the guard has been applied, the Brazilian Jiu Jitsu fighter must maintain the same relative position between himself and the opponent. He must therefore follow every move the adversary makes, insuring that his presently secured position is not jeopardized. To fully control your opponent's body movements,

you must make at least one of his arms weak and incapable of changing positions.
4. In order to achieve the above principle, it is essential that the Brazilian Jiu Jitsu fighter's posture on the mat be poised and flexible.
5. Never persist with a control position when the arms and legs have been partially compromised. Change to another type of guard or break away. Reposition yourself as soon as you realize that you do not have complete control of your opponent's movements. Remember, this control will open the doors for the final submission technique.
6. Always be watching for the opportunity in applying a chokehold, arm-lock or leg-lock, because in the course of your opponent's struggles he just may give you the opening you require.

Types of Guard

As mentioned in the beginning, the fundamental guard is referred as "close guard." Ability, strength or size of an opponent, better suits us to open our legs and control that opponent's movement, by placing our feet in his hips and hooking his knees. This is commonly called "open guard." When we use our feet to block our opponent's arms by either pressing against his shoulders or biceps as we grab his sleeves, we will be using a "spider guard" approach. These two different types of guards can be categorized under the "open guard" concept. Since our guard is opened and not closed, it is the details and intrinsic maneuvers that separate them in their own division.

When an opponent's legs are trapped by our two legs, it is called "half guard." The name is called and defined as "half guard" for the simple reason there is only one of the opponent's legs placed inside and under controlled by our two legs. One leg out and one leg in. It is a transitory phase between the close guard and then the final passing of the guard to gain the side control of your opponent.

The final guard position is called "butterfly." This guard gets its name from the position our legs are in when both feet are inside the opponent's legs. The legs are close to the groin with the opponent's body either straight or slightly leaning forward. At first sight, our feet seem to be trapped between the opponent's legs and to a certain extent, this is true. Many reversals and sweeps can be applied easily if we have proper knowledge of leverage and balance when our opponent's body is in this position. The correct use of our knees and shins play a very important role in the mastery of this type of guard, especially when combined with one leg outside of the opponent's body.

Introduction

Hip Movement

The proper use of the hip is essential in the development of a correct guard. The right positioning of the hip will affect how you can move your trunk and legs and control the opponent's weight. It is also effective when applying any submission technique from the guard. Keep in mind the hip is the part of your body that connects the trunk with the legs. Specific exercises and drills that help develop hip movement should be addressed in all training sessions. Only after the practitioner has developed a high level of 'loose' movement in the hips, will he then be able to incorporate actual attacking techniques into his game. The secret in applying a submission technique during a sparring match lies in the ability of being able to set the hip in the right position without letting the opponent know.

An important point to note when keeping your hips ready to move at all times is that the upper part of your back and the supporting point of your legs [floor or opponent's body] should be realized. These two will determine the amount of movement you will have when trying to perform submissions and guard replacements. Those two points will allow you to 'lift' the hips from the floor and re-adjust your position preventing the opponent in passing your guard.

Elements of Control

It should be understood that is practically impossible to keep a skilled opponent inside your close guard all the time. Therefore, there are other elements that will help you keep the opponent under your control. For one, there is the grip on the opponent's gi. The basic grip is the hand grabbing one side of the opponent's inside collar. This grip should be strong and committed. A good collar grip will 'block' in and around 70% of all possibilities when the opponent tries to pass the guard position. Make sure your hand goes all the way to the back of his neck and that you put additional pressure by pushing with your forearm. This is a very uncomfortable position for the individual inside the guard and by pulling from this grip, you can control his upper body at will.

The second element of control is the free hand that you are not using to grab the opponent's collar. This hand is supposed to be deceiving while looking for changes and opening doors for attacks. You can go from the simplest action by trying to choke the opponent out directly, or you can choose for other and more sophisticated moves. If you decide to grab his sleeve, make sure you use the proper grip never using your thumb, it may lead to a broken finger. Another effective move is to grab the opponent's pants at the knee level. This grip is very important if we are planning to apply sweeps and reversals.

The final element of control is the hip. As already stated, the hips play a very important role in maintaining a tight control over your opponent. Keep the hips relaxed, but firm. Don't be afraid of opening your legs to fight from an open guard position if you feel the opponent is going to break your guard, gaining an advantageous position.

Replacing the Guard

Technically, you should only open your legs when you can't keep the opponent inside of your guard. This will set up a new state and for a few seconds you may lose control of the situation. It is here when the concept of 'replacing' the guard appears. Make sure your hip and body movements are relaxed enough to immediately re-assume a new position by using your arms and legs, stopping the opponent from making the pass of the guard a reality. By your hands pushing the opponent away, it will give you the necessary time and space to re-adjust and re-position your body to maintain control. It is at this moment when the opponent is more susceptible in being countered by sweeps and reversals.

In the next chapters to come, you will find a series of technical combinations that are to be used from the different types of guard positions. Study them carefully and remember, basic foundation is what it takes to become effective in using these effective techniques.

When training at the school, forget the competition and solely aim to be efficient, even if it means performing techniques and movements in which you are not skillful. Jiu Jitsu's legacy is always to emerge victorious from a fight. The Jiu Jitsu practitioner's goal is to emerge from battle the victor and in real circumstances "being off your guard" is your greatest enemy.

To endure the journey, one must find the enjoyment and humor within the process. Like art, Jiu Jitsu is a painting with many strokes that in the end will unveil a masterpiece. Have fun with your training!

THE CLOSE GUARD

Technique 1 2	Technique 16 40
Technique 2 4	Technique 17 44
Technique 3 6	Technique 18 46
Technique 4 10	Technique 19 48
Technique 5 14	Technique 20 52
Technique 6 16	Technique 21 54
Technique 7 18	Technique 22 58
Technique 8 20	Technique 23 60
Technique 9 22	Technique 24 62
Technique 10 24	Technique 25 66
Technique 11 26	Technique 26 68
Technique 12 28	Technique 27 70
Technique 13 30	Technique 28 72
Technique 14 32	Technique 29 76
Technique 15 36	Technique 30 80

TECHNIQUE 1
THE CLOSE GUARD

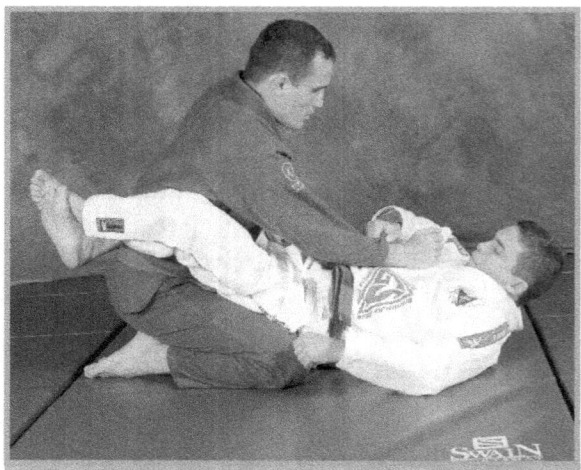

1. Gerson has his opponent inside his guard and under control.

2. He reaches out with his left hand and grabs the opponent's pant on the right side as he simultaneously controls his opponent's right arm with a grip on the sleeve.

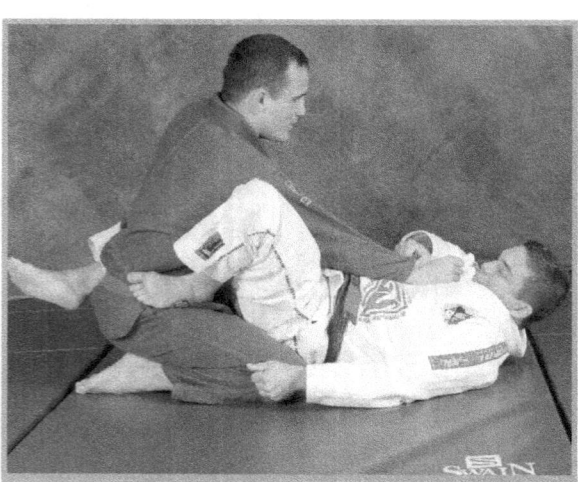

3. He moves his left foot and places it on the opponent's right hip,

4. then brings his own hips up as he supports himself, using the opponent's right hip and his own left shoulder as he passes his right leg over the opponent's head and places it on his right shoulder.

5. Gerson moves to the left and brings his right leg over his opponent's head, and putting his right knee on the ground,

6. he brings his hips forward to control the action as he firmly secures the opponent's right arm.

7. Then, he turns to the right side and begins to adopt a side position.

8. Finally, he moves his body completely to the side and brings his left arm under the opponent's head for complete side control.

TECHNIQUE 2
THE CLOSE GUARD

1. Gerson has his opponent inside his guard and under control.

2. He reaches with his left hand and grabs the opponent's pant on the right side as he simultaneously controls his opponent's right arm with a grip on the sleeve.

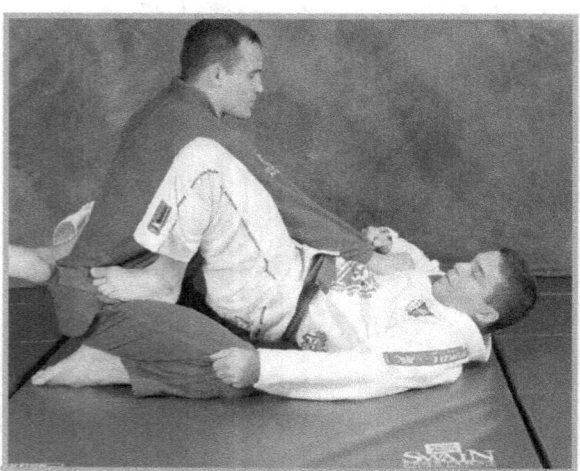

3. He moves his left foot and places it on the opponent's right hip,

4. then brings his own hips up as he supports himself, using the opponent's right hip and his own left shoulder as he passes his right leg over the opponent's head and places it on his right shoulder.

5. Gerson moves to the left and brings his right leg over his opponent's head and puts his right knee on the ground.

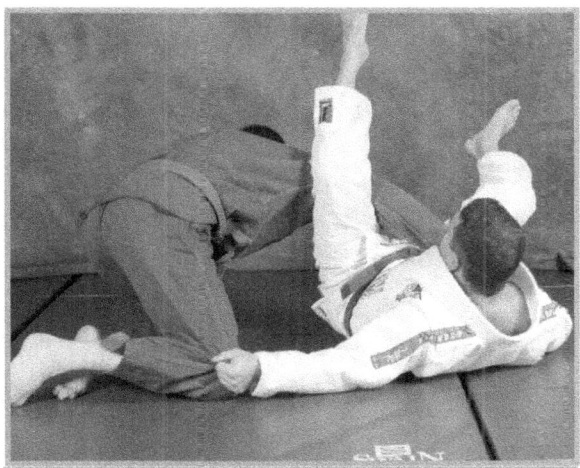

6. This time, the opponent feels the intention and blocks the action by moving slightly forward. Gerson reacts by moving his hips to the right and pushing in the same direction.

7. Then, he lands in the perfect position to...

8. turn his body to the right and apply an *omoplata*.

TECHNIQUE 3
THE CLOSE GUARD

1. Gerson has the opponent inside his guard and under control.

2. The opponent starts his action by bringing his left knee up, but Gerson reacts by getting a double grip on the opponent's right sleeve.

3. The opponent stands up completely...

4. and Gerson releases the grip of his left hand to pass his left arm inside the opponent's left leg to secure the grip on the right sleeve again.

5. Keeping a firm and secure grip that controls the left leg and right arm of his opponent, Gerson brings up his right hand and grabs the opponent's right collar...

6. then, he opens his guard and brings his left leg over the opponent's right arm...

(CONTINUED ON NEXT PAGE)

TECHNIQUE 3 (CONTINUED)

(CONTINUED FROM PREVIOUS PAGE)

7. and brings him down to the ground...

8. where he keeps pushing forward...

9. forcing the opponent to roll and turn to the right...

10. where Gerson slides his body to the left...

11. and mounts his opponent without releasing the grips...

12. for a complete mount control.

TECHNIQUE 4

THE CLOSE GUARD

1. Gerson has the opponent inside his guard and grabs the collar with his right hand and the opponent's right sleeve with the left hand.

2. The opponent starts his attack by lifting his left knee up...

3. and then his right knee to stand up completely.

4. Gerson doesn't release the grips and keeps his guard closed which for the opponent to lifting him up.

5. Gerson release the left hand grip and passes his left hand under the opponent's right arm.

6. Then, he does the same with his right hand and keeps his body close to the opponent's chest.

7. Immediately, he drops his legs to the ground and brings his hip back...

(CONTINUED ON NEXT PAGE)

TECHNIQUE 4 (CONTINUED)

(CONTINUED FROM PREVIOUS PAGE)

8. to create a solid base...

9. to insert his right leg over the opponent's left leg and throw him to the ground...

10. where he can control him and begin to attack from inside the guard.

TECHNIQUE 5
THE CLOSE GUARD

1. Gerson has his opponent inside his guard and controls both sleeves with a double grip.

2. The opponent starts his action by bringing his left knee up…

3. and then does the same with the right knee.

4. Gerson, without letting go the grip of the sleeve, slides both of his legs along the opponent's thighs…

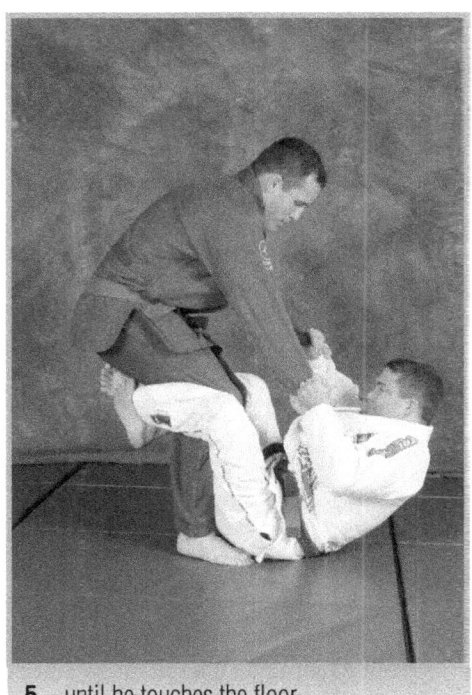

5. until he touches the floor.

6. Then, with both legs, he squeezes the opponent's legs as he simultaneously brings him out of balance by using the grips on the sleeves.

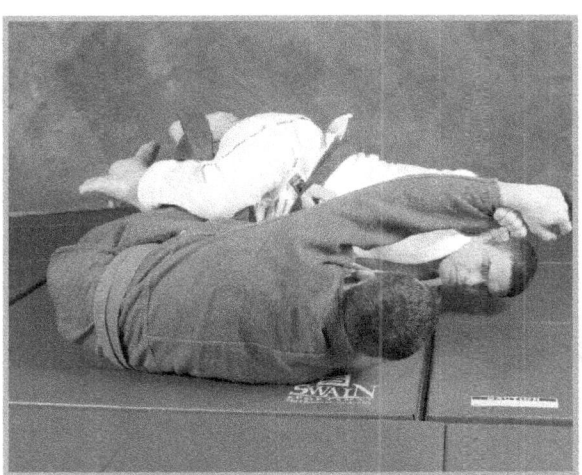

7. He pushes [with his legs] and pulls [with the hands] to the left and brings the opponent to the ground...

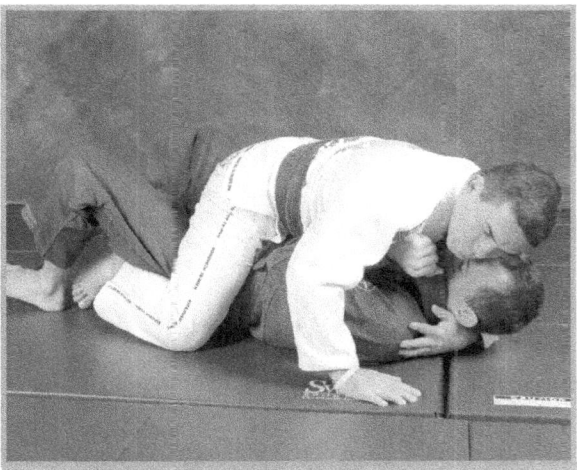

8. where he applies a full mount position for complete control before initiating his attack.

TECHNIQUE 6

THE CLOSE GUARD

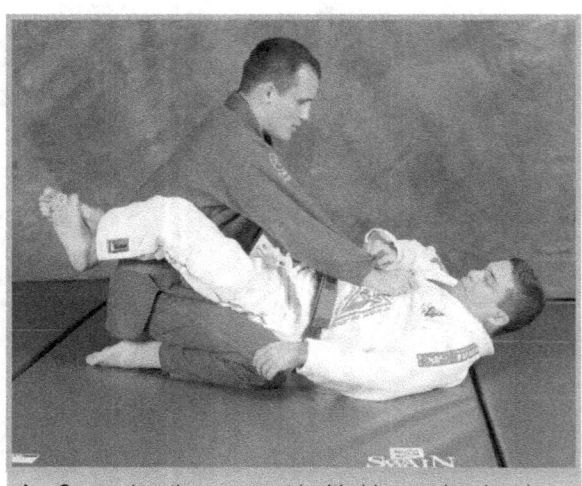

1. Gerson has the opponent inside his guard and under control.

2. The opponent starts his action by bringing his left knee up, but Gerson reacts by securing the grip of his right hand.

3. Then, the opponent brings his right knee up and Gerson reacts by passing his left arm under the opponent's left leg,

4. then brings his own right arm over to create a support base…

5. from where he will be able to sweep his opponent...

6. to the ground.

7. Then, he moves his hips forward, grabs his opponent's head and, applying pressure,

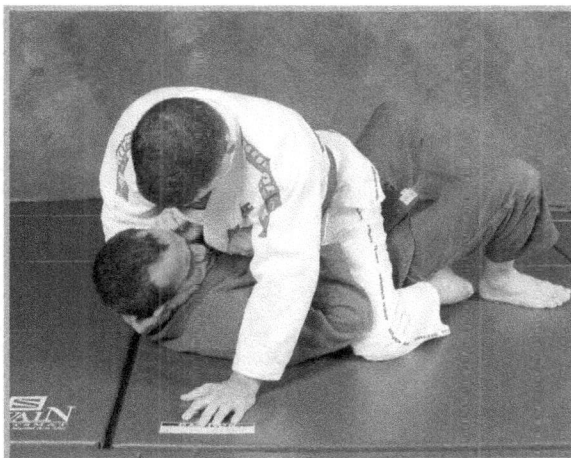

8. controls the opponent with a full mount position.

TECHNIQUE 7

THE CLOSE GUARD

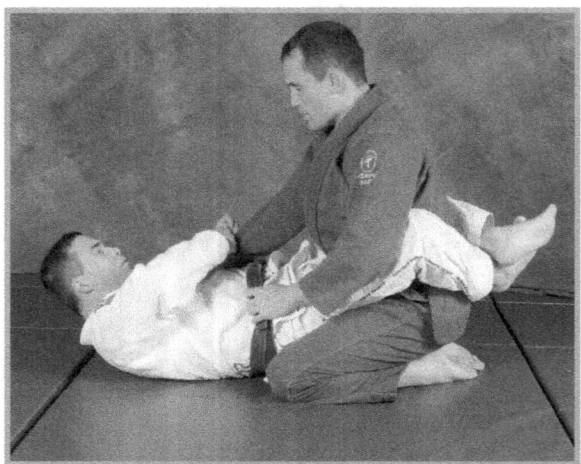

1. Gerson has the opponent inside his guard and under control.

2. The opponent starts his action by bringing his left knee up and Gerson reacts by securing the grip of his right hand.

3. Then, the opponent brings his right knee up and Gerson passes his left arm under the opponent's left leg,

4. and brings his own right arm over to create a support base...

5. so he can turn around and begin to...

6. unbalance his opponent...

7. who leans forward and prevents Gerson's attacking action.

8. Gerson then changes his plan and grabs his opponent's right leg,

9. taking him down to the ground...

10. and beginning his attack from the inside of the half-guard.

TECHNIQUE 8

THE CLOSE GUARD

1. Gerson has the opponent inside of his closed guard.

2. He moves his right hand and grabs the opponent's left pant at the level of the knee.

3. From there, he opens his guard and gets momentum to…

4. sweep his opponent by using the pull of the left hand, which is grabbing the opponent's right sleeve, the push of the right leg, and the pull of his right hand holding the opponent's pants.

5. Then, he mounts the opponent for full control as he passes his left arm under the opponent's head for better balance.

TECHNIQUE 9

THE CLOSE GUARD

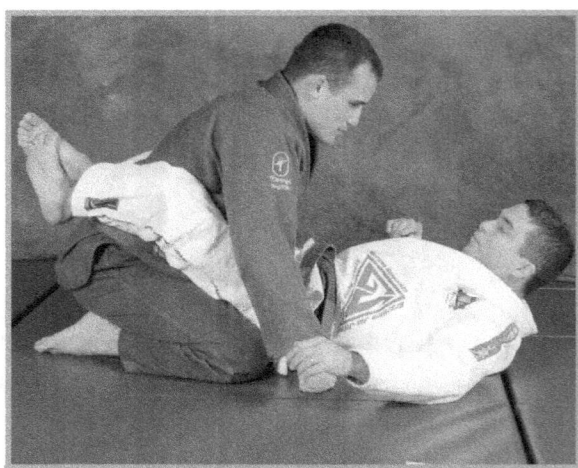

1. Gerson has the opponent under control inside of his closed guard.

2. As he controls the opponent's right arm by grabbing the wrist with his left hand, Gerson opens the guard and plant the right foot on the floor to establish his base.

3. Then, he moves to the left and supports his body by putting his left forearm on the ground.

4. Moving his right hand over the opponent's right shoulder...

5. he reaches all the way and traps the opponent's right arm.

6. Then, Gerson starts to move to the left as he brings his left leg close to the opponent's right thigh…

7. and keeping his body close to him, sweeps him and…

8. ends up on top with complete control from the mount position.

TECHNIQUE 10

THE CLOSE GUARD

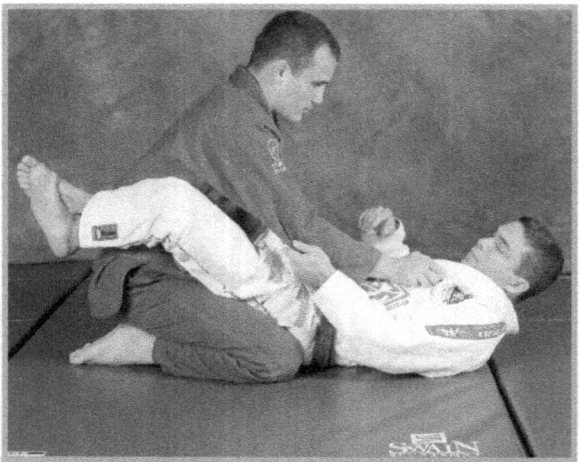

1. Gerson has the opponent under control inside of his closed guard and grabs the opponent's right sleeve with his left hand.

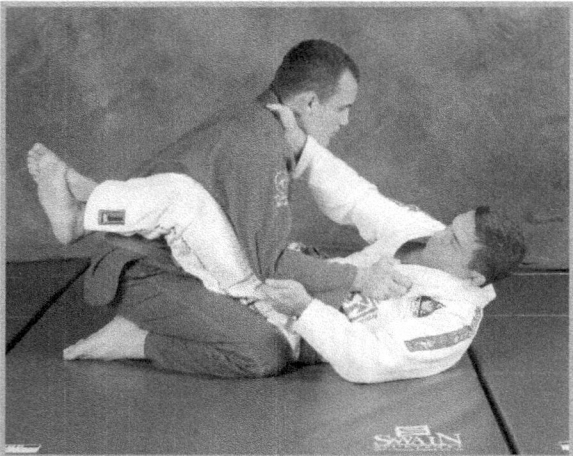

2. Then, he brings his right hand to the opponent's right side of the collar...

3. and opens his guard...

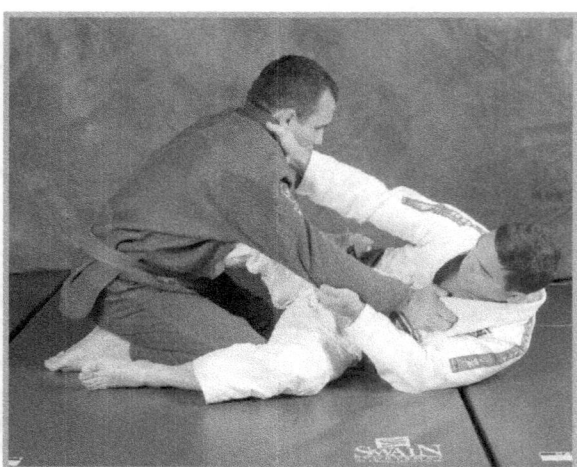

4. so he can bring his left leg to the ground, close to the opponent's right thigh.

5. Now, Gerson slides his body to the left and creates a base...

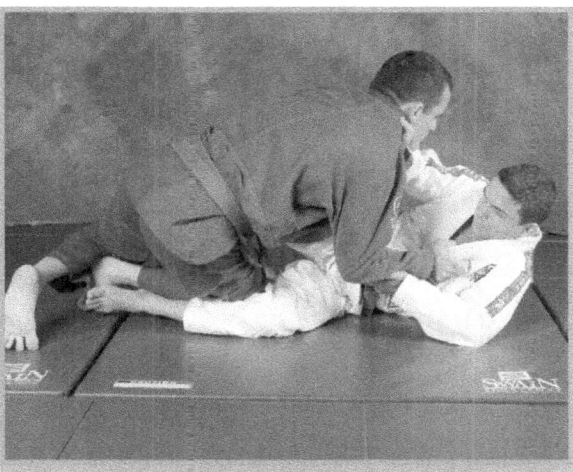

6. to unbalance the opponent by pulling with his left hand and pushing with his right shin toward the left side...

7. which sweeps the opponent onto the ground,

8. where Gerson mounts him for a full control position.

TECHNIQUE 11
THE CLOSE GUARD

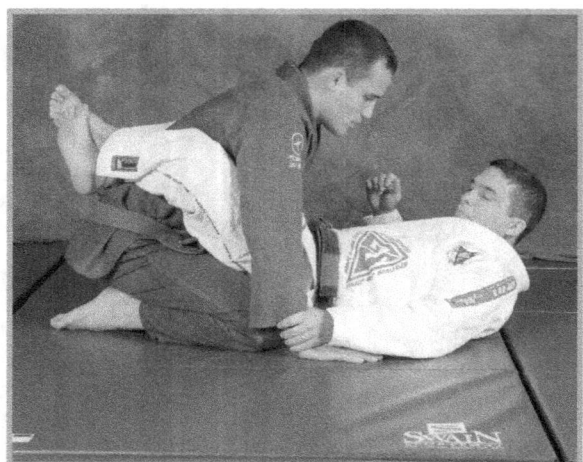

1. Gerson has the opponent inside of his closed guard and controls the opponent's right arm by grabbing the wrist with his left hand.

2. Gerson opens the guard and plants the right foot on the floor to establish his base,

3. as he reaches over the opponent's right shoulder…

4. to grab his own left wrist.

5. Once he has a tight grip of his own left wrist, he squeezes hard

6. and moves his body to the right so he ends on his back, to apply a kimura armlock.

TECHNIQUE 12
THE CLOSE GUARD

1. Gerson has the opponent inside of his closed guard and controls the opponent's right arm by grabbing the sleeve with his left hand.

2. Then, he brings his right hand and controls the opponent right elbow by holding the right forearm with his right hand on the outside part of the opponent's elbow.

3. Gerson brings his left foot and places it on the opponent's right hip to prevent the opponent from moving away.

4. Sliding his body to the right, Gerson brings his right leg toward the opponent's left armpit...

5. and passes his left leg to the front, placing it on the left side of the opponent's neck...

6. and squeezes hard as he simultaneously lifts his hips up to apply a painful armlock.

TECHNIQUE 13

THE CLOSE GUARD

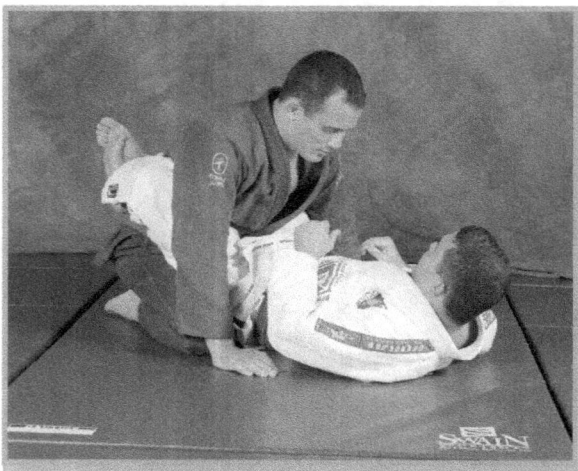

1. Gerson has the opponent inside of his closed guard.

2. Then, he brings his right hand under the opponent's left arm...

3. as he opens his guard and slides to the side to create space...

4. so he can pull the opponent's left arm to the front as...

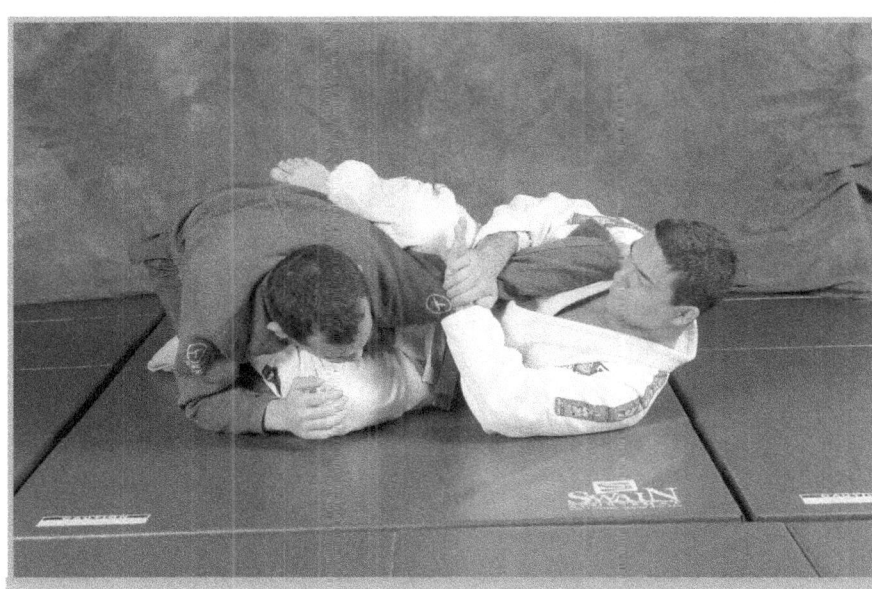

5. he simultaneously controls the opponent's body with his legs.

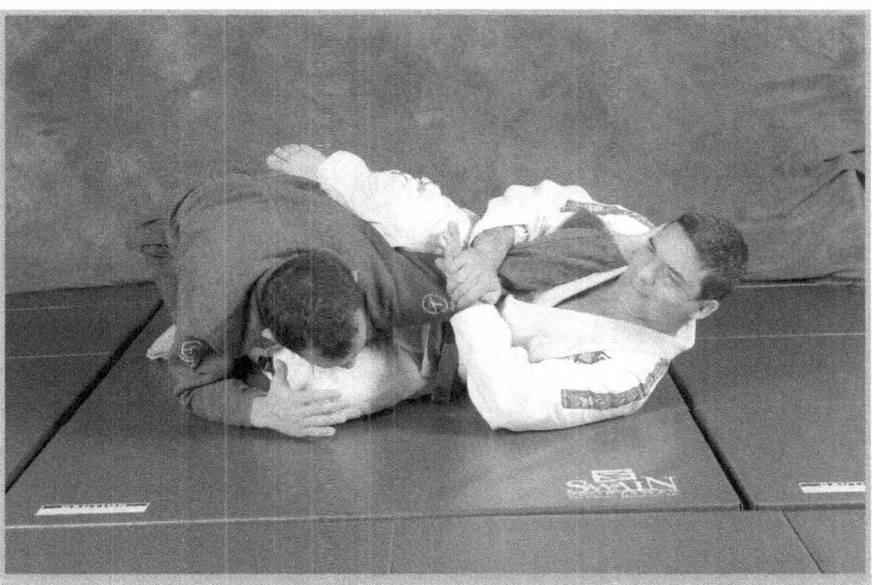

6. Once the position is secured, Gerson applies pressure on the elbow joint and finishes with a straight armlock.

TECHNIQUE 14

THE CLOSE GUARD

1. Gerson has the opponent inside of his closed guard and controls the opponent's left arm by grabbing the sleeve with his right hand.

2. He reaches to control the elbow to attack the left arm,

3. but the opponent blocks the action by leaving his right arm on the side.

4. Gerson slides his body to the left and brings his left leg up,

5. trying to get an armlock that the opponent stops by moving his trunk up.

6. Immediately, Gerson turns around, grabs the opponent's belt on the back, moves his left leg to the side…

7. and sits up…

8. so he can change the attack to an *omoplata*.

(CONTINUED ON NEXT PAGE)

TECHNIQUE 14 (CONTINUED)

(CONTINUED FROM PREVIOUS PAGE)

9. As soon as the opponent feels the omoplata attack,

10. he turns around facing Gerson.

11. This places him in a perfect position for Gerson to close the space on the right side by bringing his leg up…

12. and then reaching for his right foot with his left hand as he passes the left leg over,

13. to apply a devastating triangle choke from the guard.

TECHNIQUE 15

THE CLOSE GUARD

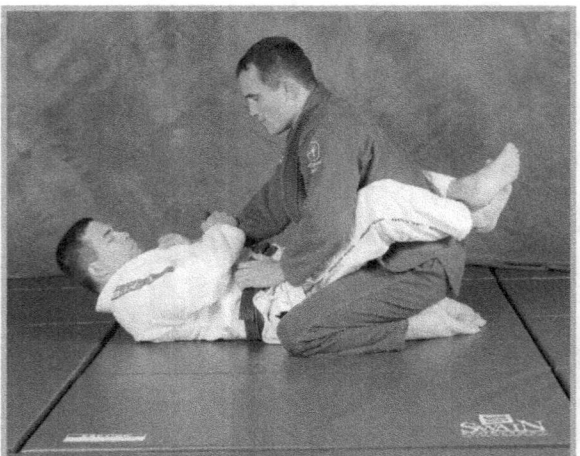

1. Gerson has the opponent inside of his closed guard and controls the opponent's right arm by grabbing the sleeve with his left hand.

2. He brings his right hand to the side and applies a double grip to the opponent's right sleeve.

3. Then, he pulls to the right side, which brings the opponent out of balance.

4. By opening his legs, Gerson allocates space to move his body to the left…

5. to reach and grab the opponent's belt from the back.

(CONTINUED ON NEXT PAGE)

TECHNIQUE 15 (CONTINUED)

(CONTINUED FROM PREVIOUS PAGE)

6. By using the right hand grip, the grip on the belt, and by leaning on his right knee,

7. Gerson establish his position so he can...

8. mount the opponent from the back.

9. Then, he allows his body to roll down and applies a choke from behind.

TECHNIQUE 16

THE CLOSE GUARD

1. Gerson has the opponent inside of his closed guard and controls the opponent's right arm by grabbing the sleeve with his left hand.

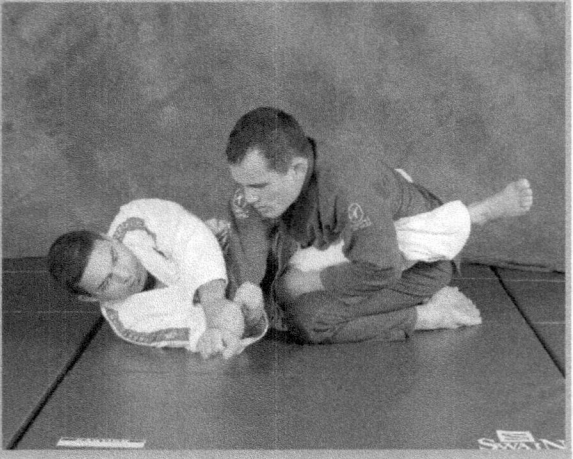

2. Then, he pulls to the right side, which brings the opponent out of balance.

3. By opening his legs, Gerson allocate space to move his body to the left...

4. to reach and grab the opponent's belt from the back, but the opponent grabs Gerson's pants and prevents Gerson from going on his back.

5. Gerson then starts to move to the side…

(CONTINUED ON NEXT PAGE)

TECHNIQUE 16 (CONTINUED)

(CONTINUED FROM PREVIOUS PAGE)

6. and brings his left hand over the opponent's neck,

7. to grab the right side of the collar as he puts pressure with his legs on the opponent's body.

8. Gerson moves backwards and lets his body roll back as he secures his grip,

9. applies pressure with the legs, and applies a choke by using the opponent's collar.

TECHNIQUE 17
THE CLOSE GUARD

1. Gerson has the opponent inside of his closed guard and controls the opponent's collar by a double grip.

2. He pulls the opponent down, close to his chest,

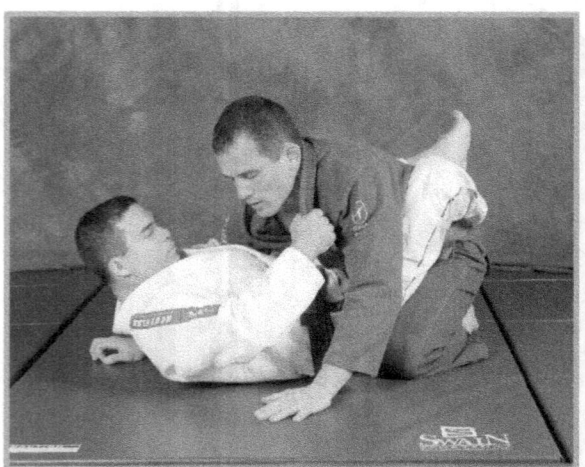

3. so he can bring his left hand over the opponent's right arm.

4. .Then, he opens up the collar with the right hand and brings his left hand…

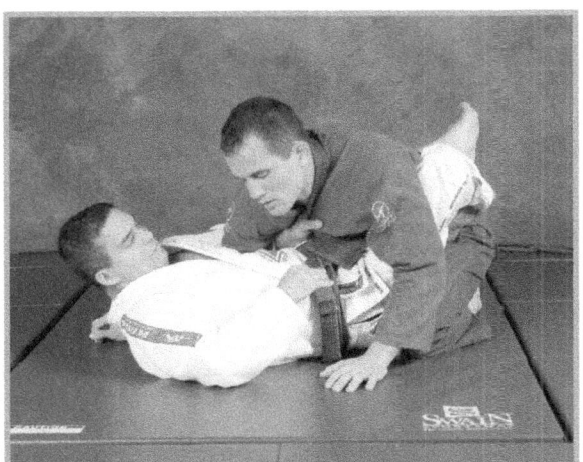

5. to control the inside of the left collar

6. Now, Gerson moves his right hand to the right side of the opponent's neck, and grabs the upper part of the collar.

7. Squeezing hard, he brings the opponent close to his chest and applies a front choke from the guard.

TECHNIQUE 18

THE CLOSE GUARD

1. Gerson has the opponent inside of his closed guard and controls the opponent's collar by a double grip.

2. He pulls the opponent down, close to his chest,

3. so he can bring his left hand over the opponent's right arm.

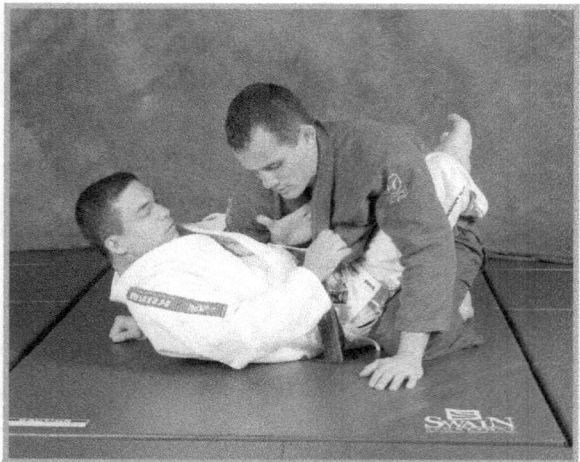

4. Then, he opens up the collar with the right hand and brings his left hand...

5. to control the inside of the left collar.

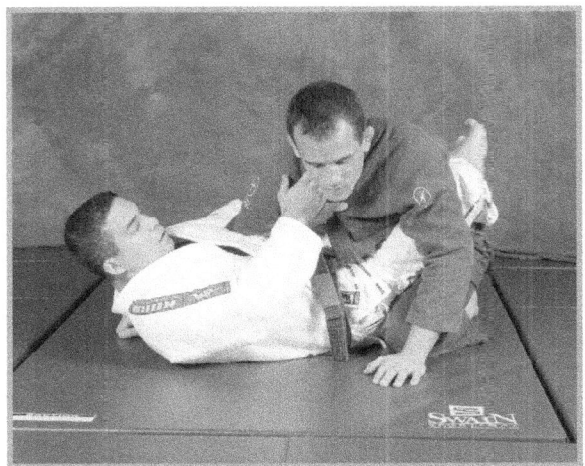

6. Then, he brings his right hand inside the opponent's collar...

7. and twists his body to the right as he applies pressure for a side choke.

TECHNIQUE 19
THE CLOSE GUARD

1. Gerson has the opponent inside of his closed guard and controls the opponent's collar by a double grip.

2. He pulls the opponent down, close to his chest,

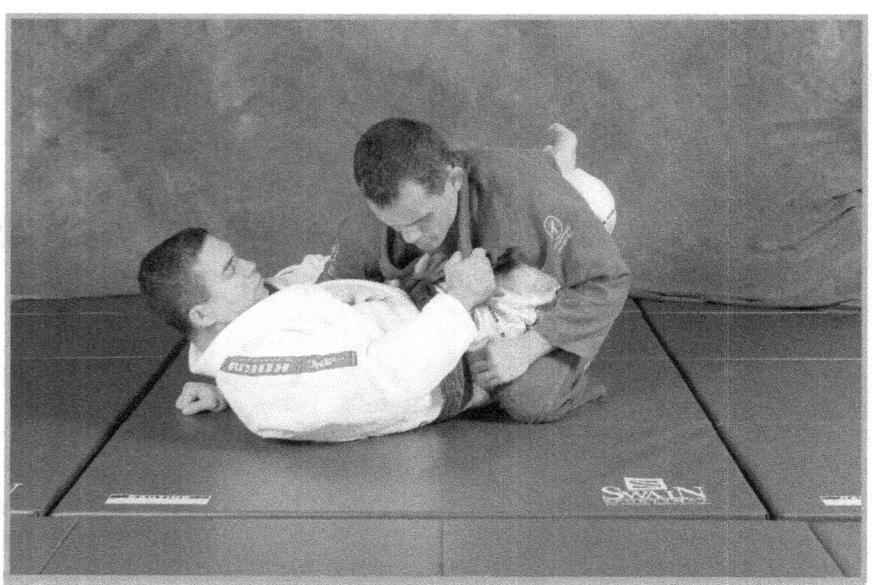

3. so he can bring his left hand over the opponent's right arm. Then, he opens up the collar with the right hand...

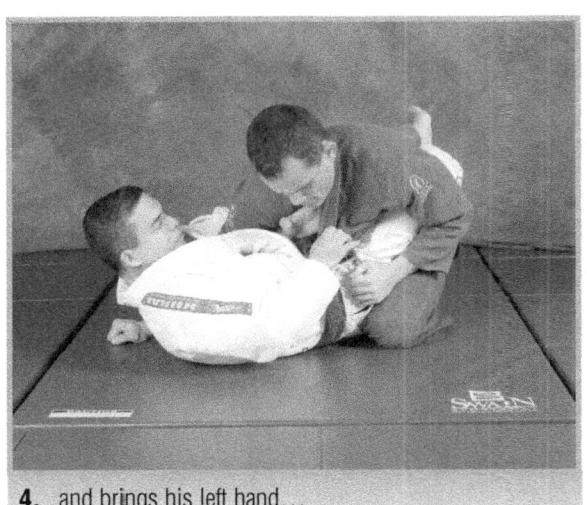
4. and brings his left hand…

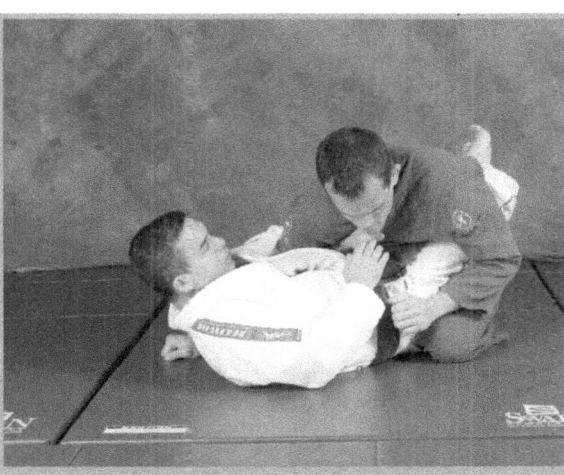
5. to control the inside of the left collar.

6. The opponent, feeling Gerson's intention to attack his neck, uses his left hand to stop Gerson's right hand from reaching the collar.

(CONTINUED ON NEXT PAGE)

TECHNIQUE 19 (CONTINUED)

(CONTINUED FROM PREVIOUS PAGE)

7. Gerson reverses the grip...

8. and moves his right leg toward the side and over the left shoulder...

9. as he simultaneously pushes his opponent's right arm to the inside and brings the left arm to the outside.

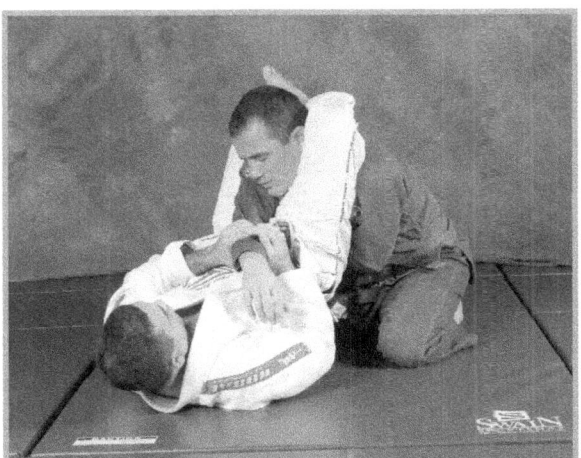

10. Now, he pulls the opponent's right arm close to his chest,

11. brings his right leg tight over the opponent's left side of the neck,

12. and applies a triangle choke to submit his opponent.

TECHNIQUE 20
THE CLOSE GUARD

1. Gerson has the opponent inside of his closed guard and controls the opponent's collar by a double grip.

2. He pulls the opponent down, close to his chest,

3. so he can bring his left hand over the opponent's right arm.

4. Then, he opens up the collar with the right hand,

5. and brings his left hand all the way inside of the opponent's collar.

6. The opponent, feeling Gerson's intention to attack his neck, moves back a little. Taking advantage of the opponent's movement, Gerson slightly pushes his opponent away to create distance,

7. brings his right foot close, and places it on the opponent's left hip as he simultaneously locks the opponent's right arm…

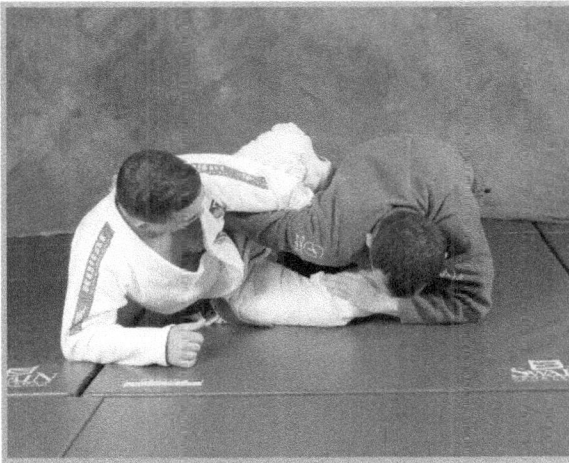

8. to apply a straight armbar by using his own body for leverage.

TECHNIQUE 21

THE CLOSE GUARD

1. Gerson has the opponent inside of his closed guard and controls the opponent's collar by a double grip.

2. He pulls the opponent down, close to his chest,

3. so he can bring his left hand over the opponent's right arm.

4. Then, he opens up the collar with the right hand,

5. and brings his left hand all the way inside the opponent's collar.

6. Gerson slightly pushes his opponent away to create distance,

(CONTINUED ON NEXT PAGE)

TECHNIQUE 21 (CONTINUED)

(CONTINUED FROM PREVIOUS PAGE)

7. then brings his right foot close and places it on the opponent's left hip as he simultaneously locks the opponent's right arm, to apply a straight armbar by using his own body for leverage.

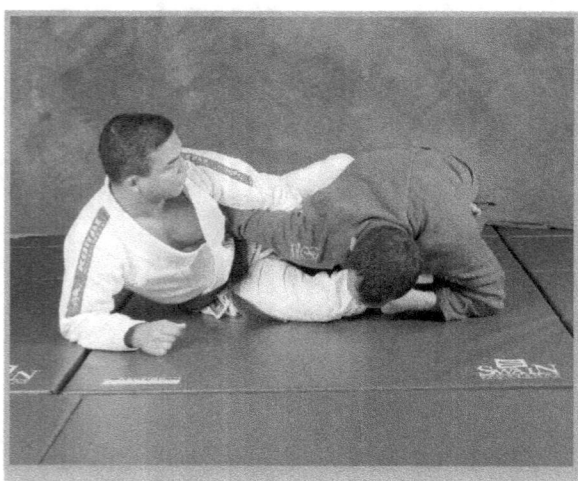

8. The opponent, feeling the pressure, bends his right arm, which nullifies the effect of the armlock, in order to escape.

9. Gerson then brings his left leg over the opponent's right arm,

10. reaches to the side with his left hand to establish a base, and slides his body backwards to bring his right leg out.

11. Then, he brings his left leg to the front, secures it with his right hand and, controlling the opponent's body with his left hand, applies an *omoplata*.

TECHNIQUE 22
THE CLOSE GUARD

1. Gerson has the opponent inside of his closed guard and controls the opponent's collar by a double grip.

2. He pulls the opponent down, close to his chest,

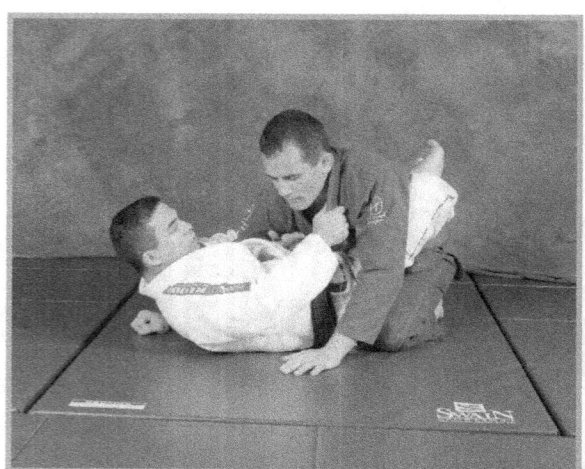

3. so he can bring his left hand over the opponent's right arm.

4. Then, he opens up the collar with the right hand...

5. and brings his left hand all the way inside of the opponent's collar.

6. The opponent brings his right elbow down and close to his body. Then, Gerson slides his right foot and places it on the opponent's left hip.

7. Gerson moves his left leg up to put additional pressure in the position and…

8. pushes with his right foot as he twists the grip of the left hand to apply a bent-arm lock.

TECHNIQUE 23
THE CLOSE GUARD

1. Gerson has the opponent inside of his closed guard and controls the opponent's collar by a double grip.

2. He pulls the opponent down, close to his chest,

3. and brings his left hand around the opponent's back of the neck...

4. to reach and grab his right sleeve.

5. Then, he brings his right forearm down...

6. and twists the arm toward the inside and in the front of the opponent's neck...

7. to apply an *ezequiel* choke.

TECHNIQUE 24
THE CLOSE GUARD

1. Gerson has the opponent inside of his closed guard.

2. The opponent initiates his action by bringing his left knee up,

3. and then the right knee to stand up.

4. He pulls hard to break free from Gerson's grip...

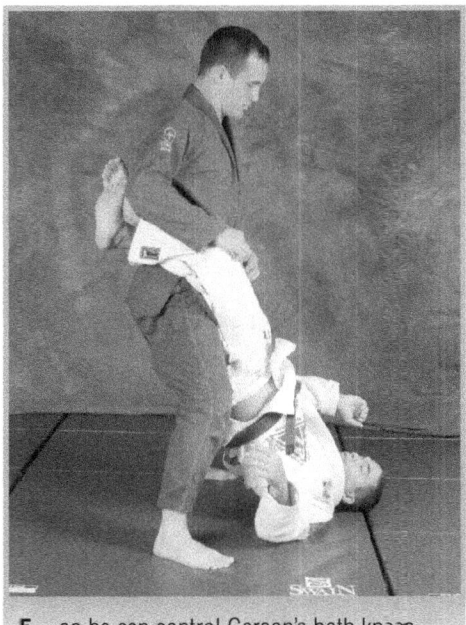

5. so he can control Gerson's both knees and...

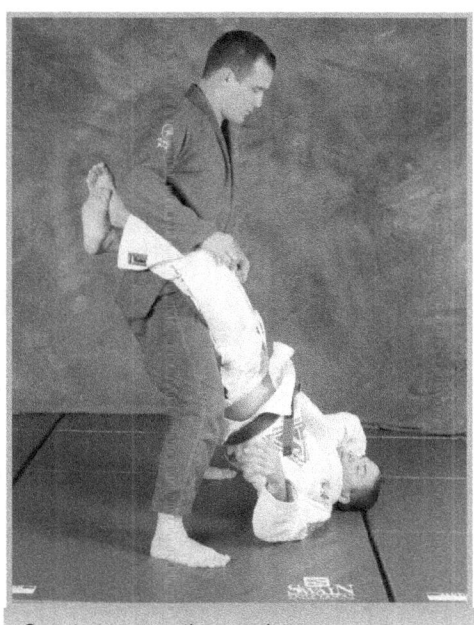

6. start to pass the guard.

7. Gerson feel the intention as he opens his guard, so he uses his right arm to pivot on his body...

8. to reach the opponent's right leg with his right hand.

(CONTINUED ON NEXT PAGE)

TECHNIQUE 24 (CONTINUED)

(CONTINUED FROM PREVIOUS PAGE)

9. Then, by controlling his opponent's right leg, Gerson pivots under the opponent's body,

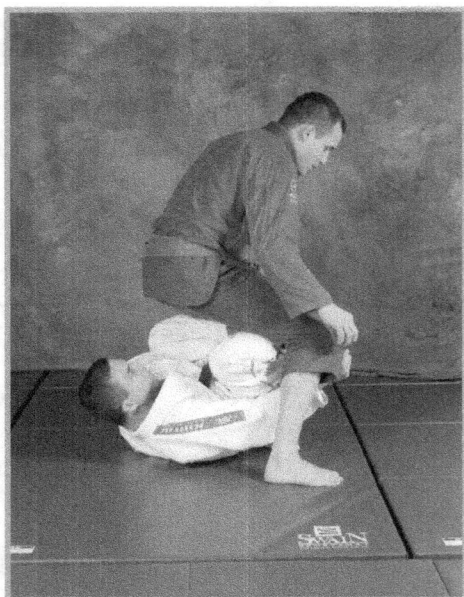

10. places himself behind the opponent, as he applies the hooks from the back,

11. and by grabbing his opponent's belt,

12. pulls him back to the ground...

13. and between his legs.

14. Once there, he secures the hooks and controls the opponent's neck,

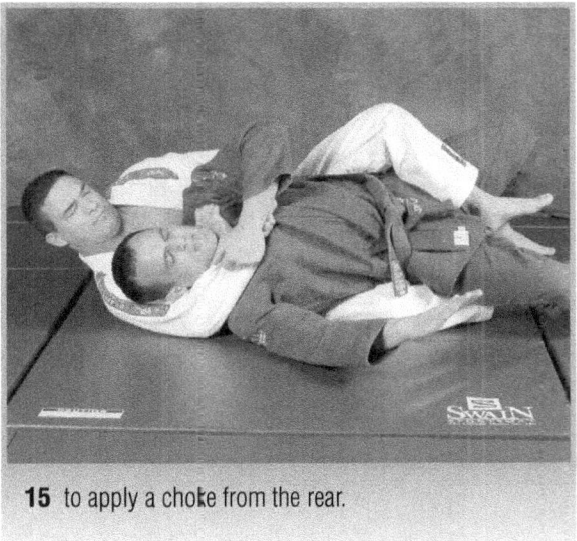

15. to apply a choke from the rear.

TECHNIQUE 25
THE CLOSE GUARD

1. Gerson has the opponent inside of his closed guard, with the right hand controlling the lapel.

2. The opponent initiates his action by bringing his left knee up,

3. and then the right knee to completely stand up.

4. He pulls hard to break free from Gerson's grip so he can control both of Gerson's knees.

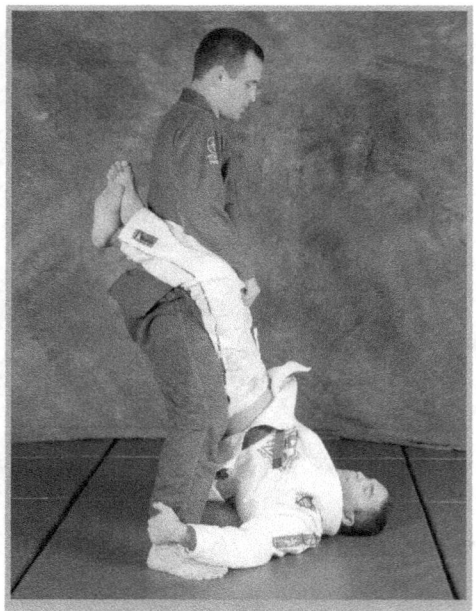

5. Gerson feels the intention, and grabs both of the opponent's ankles from behind.

6. Then, he opens the legs,

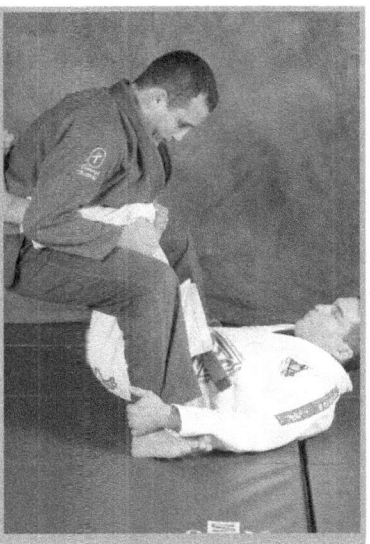

7. and pushes forward as he simultaneously pulls with both hands on the opponent's ankles…

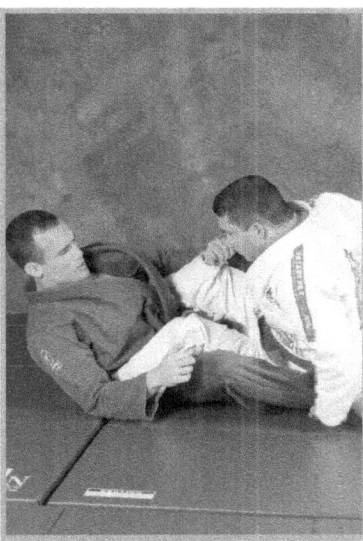

8. which brings him to the ground.

9. Gerson moves forward and keeps his hips low to apply pressure…

10. until he gets the full mounted position for a total control.

TECHNIQUE 26
THE CLOSE GUARD

1. Gerson has the opponent inside of his closed guard with a double collar control.

2. He slides his right hand all the way up to get an inside collar grip.

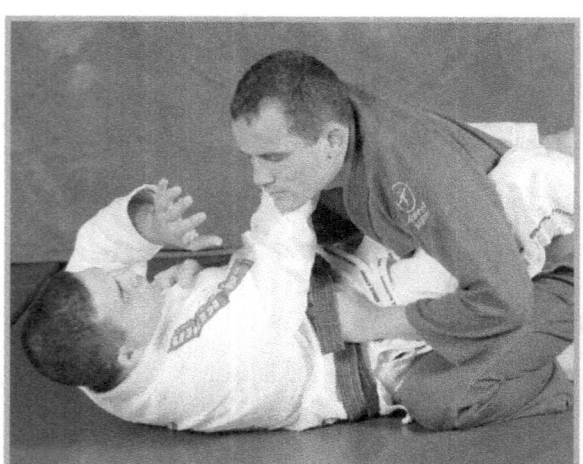

3. Then, he brings his left hand to the side,

4. to reach over the opponent's left side of the collar,

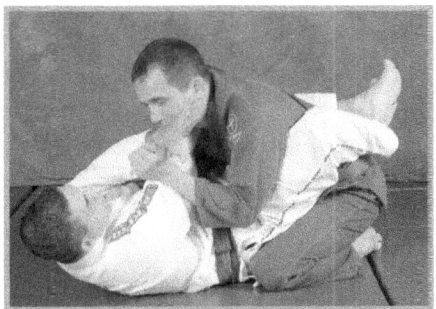

5. but the opponent stops his action.

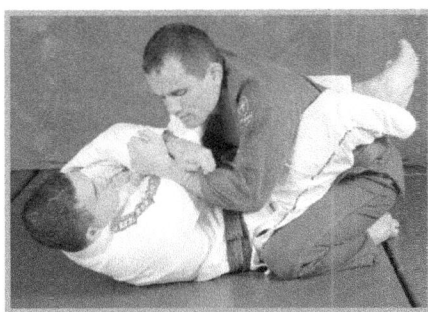

6. Gerson then reverses the grip and controls the opponent's left arm,

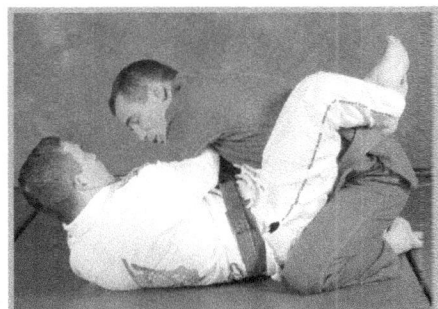

7. and pulls it toward the left side, across his own body.

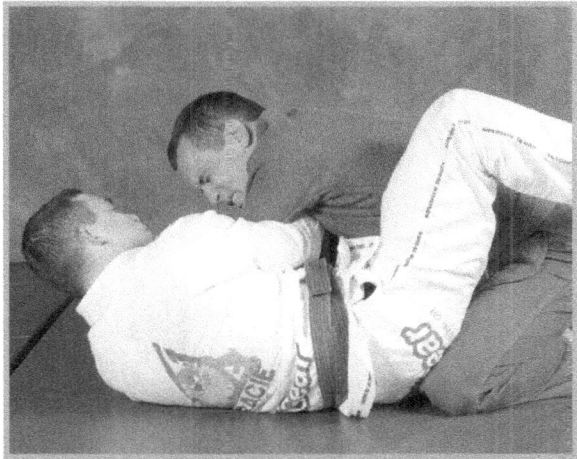

8. Gerson slides his hips to the side, squeezes hard to put pressure on the opponent's neck, using his own left arm,

9. adjusts the position, and applies a final choke.

TECHNIQUE 27
THE CLOSE GUARD

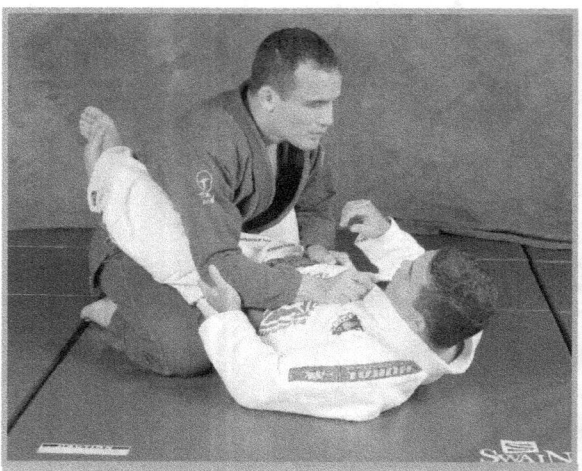

1. Gerson has the opponent inside of his closed guard.

2. He moves forward and gets a right-hand collar control.

3. He reaches over the opponent's left side of the collar,

4. but the opponent stops his action by covering with his forearm.

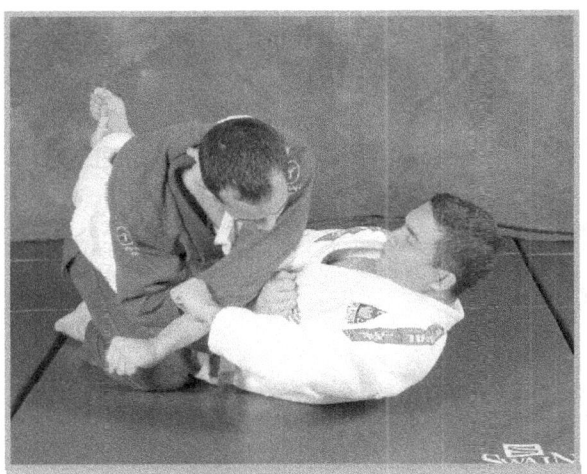

5. Gerson pulls the opponent's left arm toward the left side, across his own body.

6. Gerson slides his hips to the side and brings his leg up to create more control.

7. He puts pressure on the opponent's neck using his own left arm, adjusts the position, and applies a frontal choke.

TECHNIQUE 28
THE CLOSE GUARD

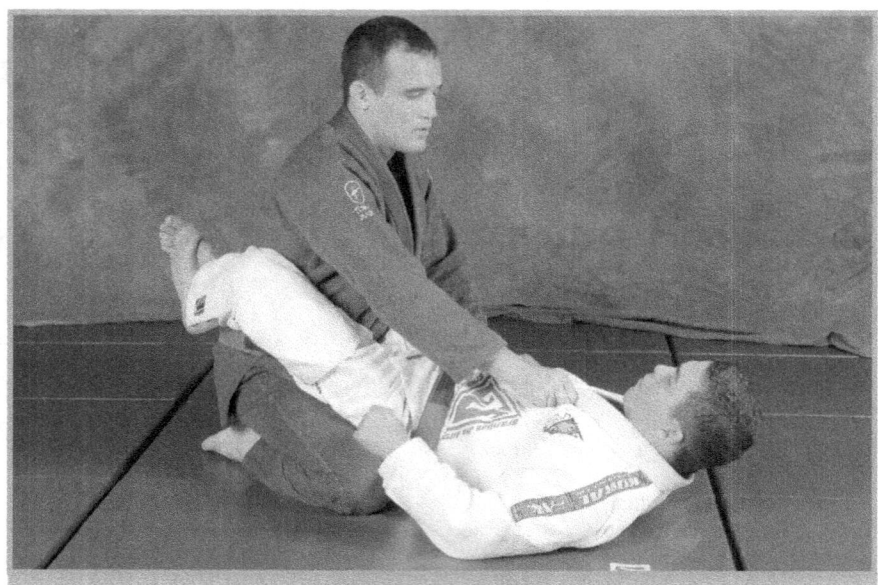

1. Gerson controls the opponent inside of his closed guard.

2. The opponent applies pressure by standing up and leaning forward with the forearm on Gerson's neck.

3. Gerson controls the action by pushing slightly away with his hip, which releases the pressure on his neck, and...

4. then allows the opponent to come forward as he moves the opponent's left arm across his body.

5. Gerson reaches out and brings his left hand to the right side…

(CONTINUED ON NEXT PAGE)

TECHNIQUE 28 (CONTINUED)

(CONTINUED FROM PREVIOUS PAGE)

6. so he can grab his own right arm.

7. Now, he opens the guard...

8. and brings the legs inside the opponent's by using the hooks.

9. Then, Gerson moves forward and pushes slightly with his legs as he applies pressure on the opponent's neck.

10. Finally, he applies pressure on the opponent's spine in combination with a frontal choke.

TECHNIQUE 29
THE CLOSE GUARD

1. Gerson has the opponent inside his closed guard.

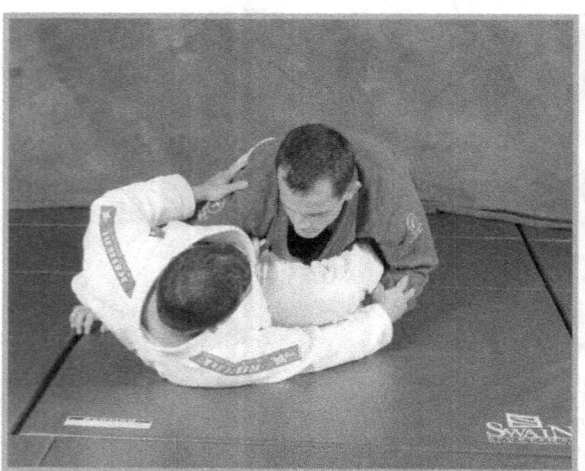

2. He opens his guard and slides his body to the left...

3. so he can start the attack for an omoplata armlock.

4. He tries to bring his left leg forward to finalize the technique,

5. but the opponent resists and…

6. ends up rolling forward to nullify the armlock attempt.

(CONTINUED ON NEXT PAGE)

TECHNIQUE 29 (CONTINUED)

(CONTINUED FROM PREVIOUS PAGE)

7. Gerson lets the body pass but stops the right leg.

8. He grabs it with both arms and places his right foot on the opponent's stomach for better control.

9. Then, he passes the opponent's leg to the left side of his body...

10. and applies pressure for the final leglock.

TECHNIQUE 30

THE CLOSE GUARD

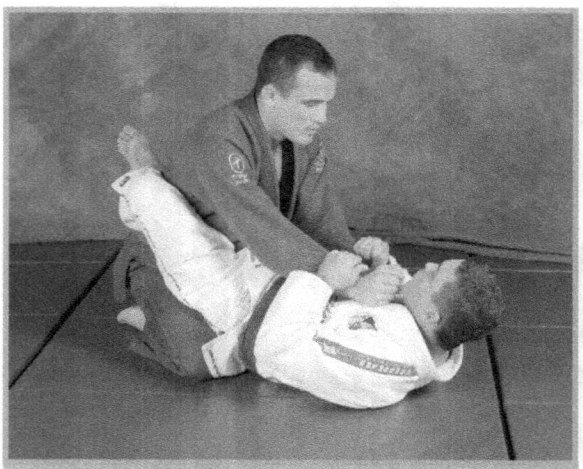

1. Gerson controls the opponent inside his closed guard.

2. He pulls his opponent closer and put both legs close to the opponent's head.

3. Maintaining the pressure with the legs, he secures the grip of both hands...

4. and applies pressure…

5. as he simultaneously lifts his hips to apply the finishing hold.

THE OPEN GUARD

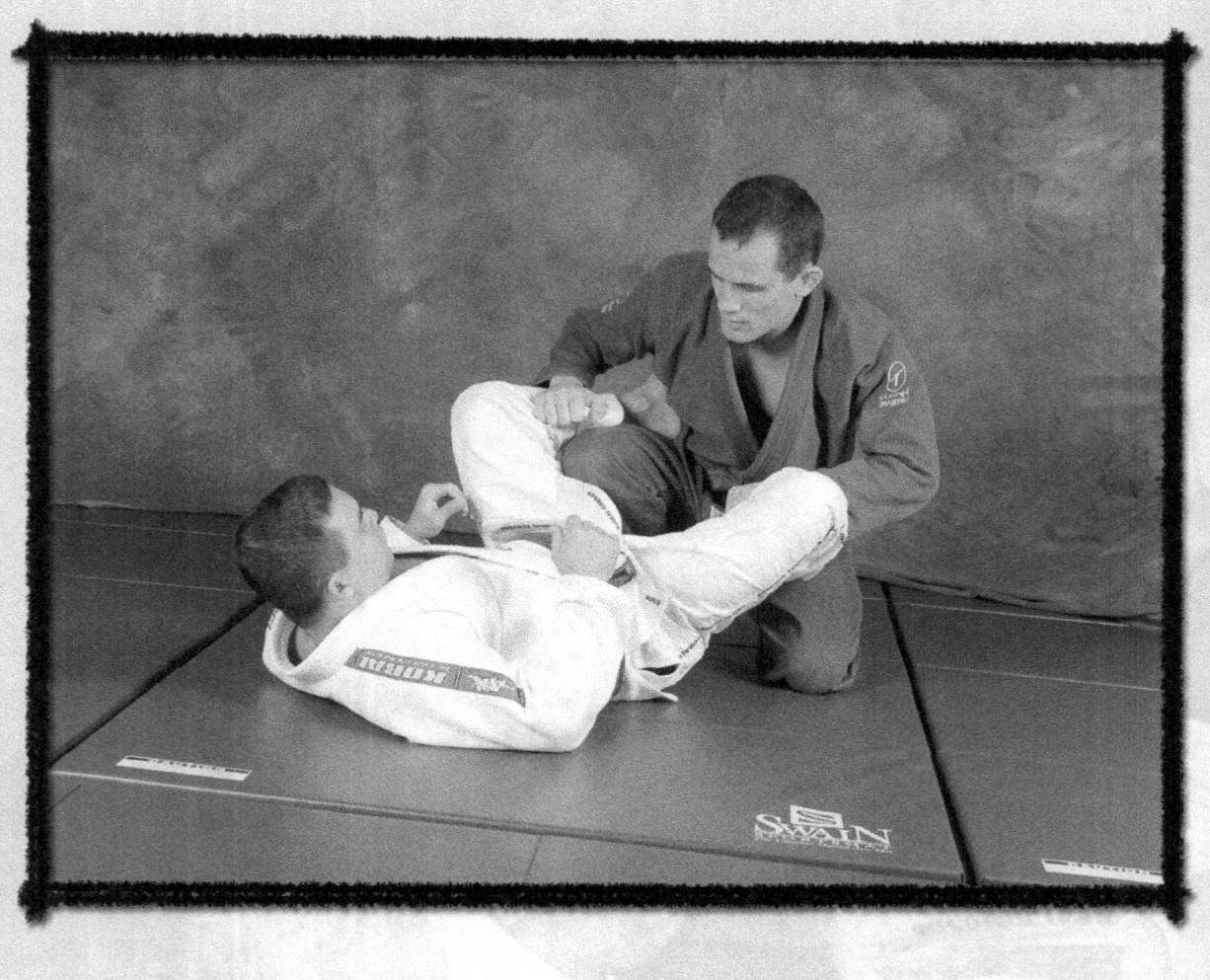

Technique 1 84	Technique 12 130
Technique 2 88	Technique 13 134
Technique 3 92	Technique 14 136
Technique 4 96	Technique 15 140
Technique 5 100	Technique 16 142
Technique 6 106	Technique 17 144
Technique 7 110	Technique 18 148
Technique 8 114	Technique 19 150
Technique 9 118	Technique 20 154
Technique 10 122	Technique 21 158
Technique 11 126	Technique 22 160

TECHNIQUE 1
THE OPEN GUARD

1. Gerson, using the open guard, faces his opponent.

2. He slides his hips back...

3. to create distance...

4. so he can open the angle

5. to bring his left hand around the opponent's body...

6. to grab the belt and secure the hooks inside the opponent's legs.

(CONTINUED ON NEXT PAGE)

TECHNIQUE 1 (CONTINUED)

THE OPEN GUARD

(CONTINUED FROM PREVIOUS PAGE)

7. Gerson then closes the distance and grabs the opponent's left arm.

8. He rolls to the side...

9. as he uses the hook of his left leg to push the opponent's body.

10. He continues rolling with his opponent…

11. and gets the mounted position for full control before initiating the attack.

TECHNIQUE 2
THE OPEN GUARD

1. The opponent is facing Gerson's open guard.

2. The opponent tries to manipulate Gerson's legs and brings the right knee to the front.

3. Gerson slides to the side and releases the grip of his right hand...

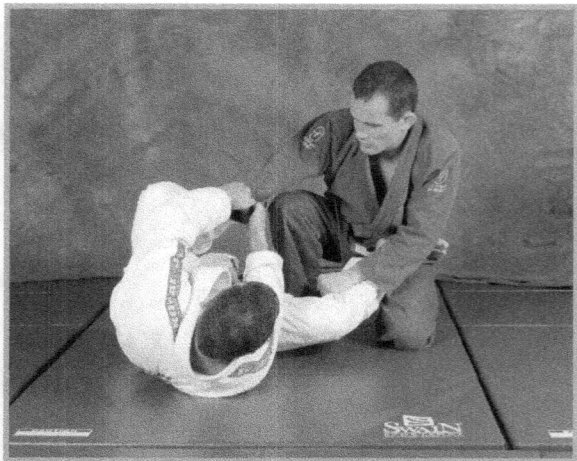

4. to grab the opponent's right sleeve.

5. Then, he moves his left leg to the side...

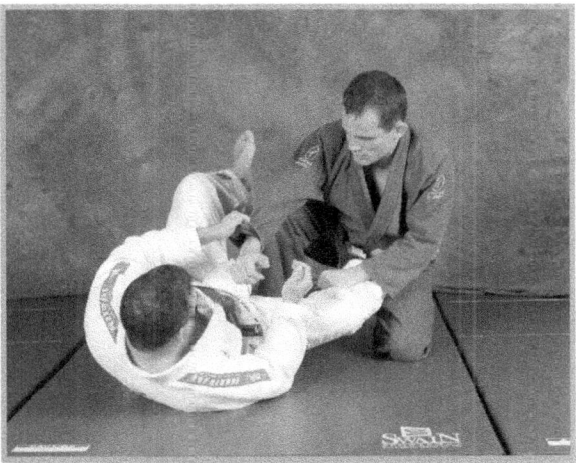
6. to create space so he can...

7. bring the left foot under the opponent's right knee,

8. as he simultaneously controls the right sleeve of the opponent's gi.

(CONTINUED ON NEXT PAGE)

TECHNIQUE 2 (CONTINUED)

THE OPEN GUARD

(CONTINUED FROM PREVIOUS PAGE)

9. Now, he brings his body up and...

10. puts the right leg outside, as he simultaneously creates leverage with his left leg.

11. He uses his left hand to help the opponent get out of balance...

12. and pulls him to the side as he sweeps him with the right leg.

13. As the opponent falls,

14. Gerson follows the action and maintains his body close to his opponent's,

15. which allows him to get up in a position of control, holding both sleeves.

16. Then, he passes to the left side,

17. where he adopts the side control to take the offensive.

TECHNIQUE 3

THE OPEN GUARD

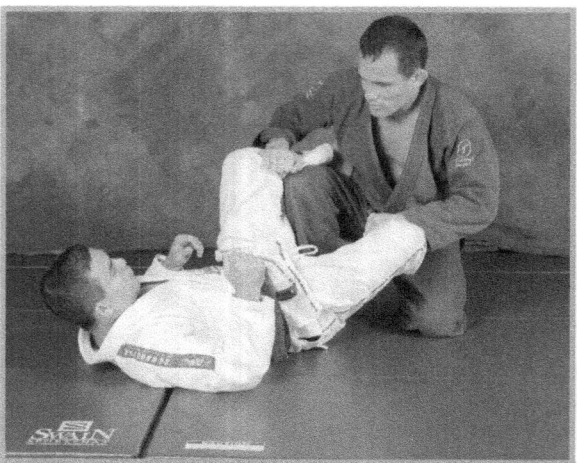

1. The opponent, facing Gerson's open guard,

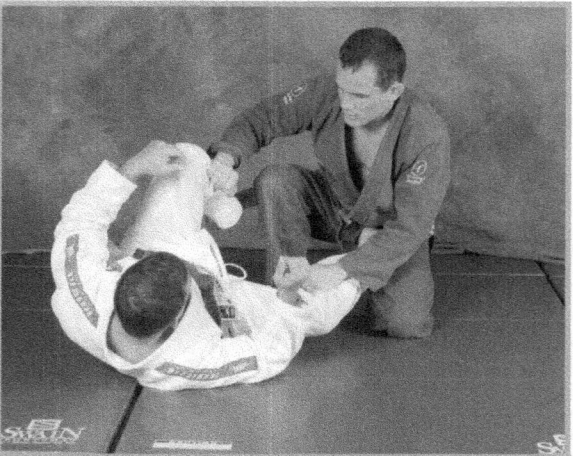

2. tries to manipulate Gerson's legs and brings his right knee to the front.

3. Gerson slides to the side and releases the grip of his right hand to grab the opponent's right sleeve.

4. Then, he moves his left leg to the side...

5. to create space so he can bring the left foot under the opponent's right knee…

6. as he simultaneously controls the right sleeve of the opponent's gi.

7. Now, he puts the right leg outside as he simultaneously creates leverage with his left leg.

8. He uses both of his hands to help the opponent get out of balance…

(CONTINUED ON NEXT PAGE)

TECHNIQUE 3 (CONTINUED)

THE OPEN GUARD

(CONTINUED FROM PREVIOUS PAGE)

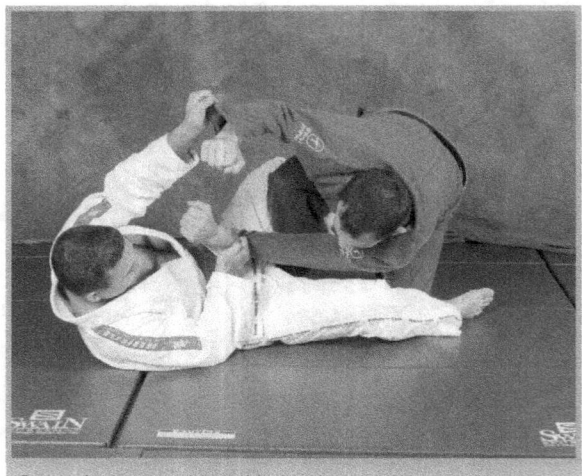

9. as he sweeps him with the right leg.

10. As the opponent falls,

11. Gerson follows the action and maintains his body close to his opponent's,

12. which allows him to get up on his knees, holding both sleeves.

13. Then, he passes to the left side, where he adopts the side control.

TECHNIQUE 4

THE OPEN GUARD

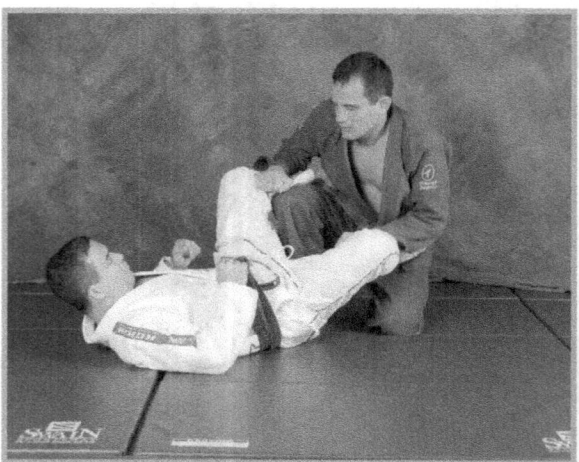

1. Gerson faces his opponent from an open guard.

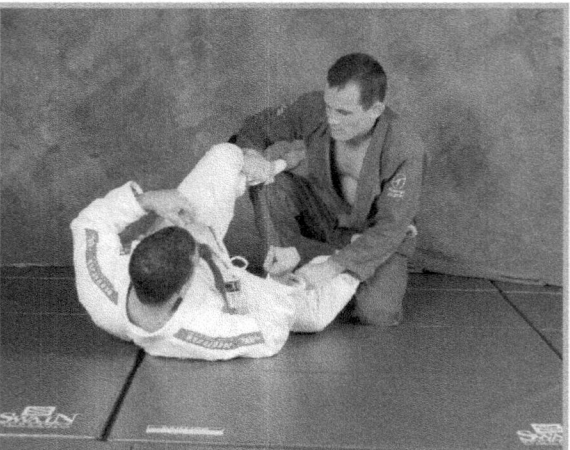

2. The opponent moves his right knee to prepare to pass the guard.

3. Gerson slides his body to the side and grabs the opponent's right sleeve with both hands.

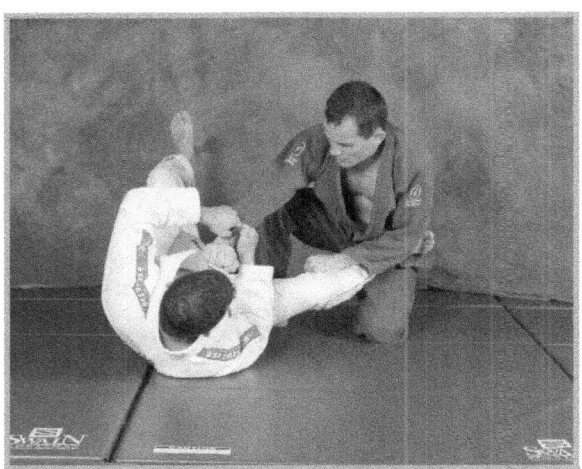
4. Then, he brings his left leg to the outside...

5. to get momentum...

6. to bring it under the opponent's right leg, as he simultaneously sits on the ground.

(CONTINUED ON NEXT PAGE)

TECHNIQUE 4 (CONTINUED)

THE OPEN GUARD

(CONTINUED FROM PREVIOUS PAGE)

7. Gerson brings his right leg down...

8. as he begins to change the grip on the opponent's right arm.

9. He passes his left arm under the opponent's right leg...

10. as reaches with his right hand to grab the opponent's left sleeve...

11. and give it to the left hand...

12. to have a secure grip holding the right leg and the left arm, using only one hand.

(CONTINUED ON NEXT PAGE)

TECHNIQUE 4 (CONTINUED)

THE OPEN GUARD

(CONTINUED FROM PREVIOUS PAGE)

13. Then, Gerson brings his right hand to the back of the opponent's collar

14. and begins to pull down...

15. until the opponent's body touches the ground...

16. completely with the left side.

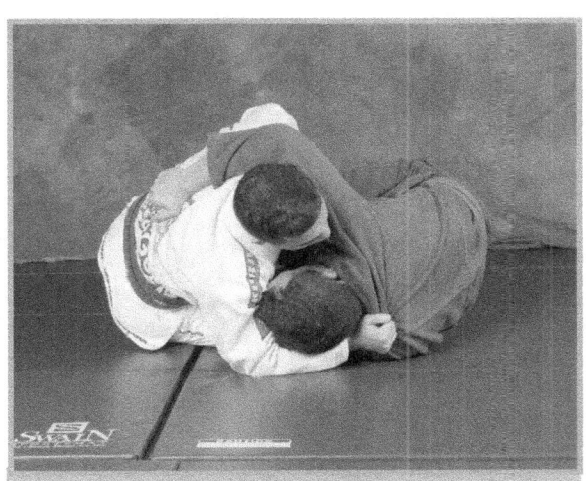

17. Gerson, without releasing the grip of the left hand,

18. adopts a side position.

19. Finally, he lets the opponent's leg and arm go,

20. and applies a full side control.

TECHNIQUE 5

THE OPEN GUARD

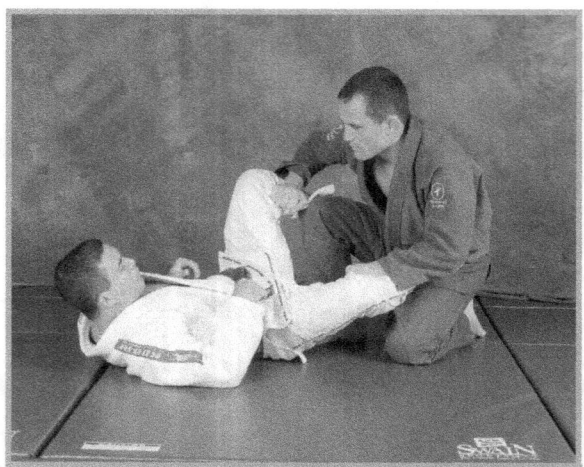

1. Gerson faces his opponent from an open guard.

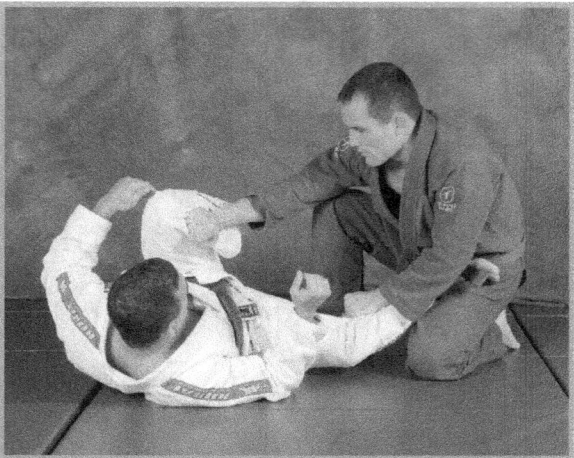

2. The opponent moves his right knee to prepare to pass the guard. Gerson slides his body to the side...

3. and grabs the opponent's right sleeve with both hands.

4. Then, he brings his left leg to the outside...

5. to get momentum...

6. to bring it under the opponent's right leg as he simultaneously sits on the ground.

7. Gerson brings his right leg down and as he grabs the opponent's left sleeve.

8. He passes his left arm under the opponent's right leg,

(CONTINUED ON NEXT PAGE)

TECHNIQUE 5 (CONTINUED)

THE OPEN GUARD
(CONTINUED FROM PREVIOUS PAGE)

9. and as he reaches with his right hand to grab the opponent's left sleeve,

10. the opponent pulls his left arm and prevents Gerson from grabbing it.

11. Gerson then moves backwards to create space,

12. and brings his right leg back.

13. He pushes with his body forward…

14. as he pulls back the opponent's right leg, which makes the opponent go to the ground.

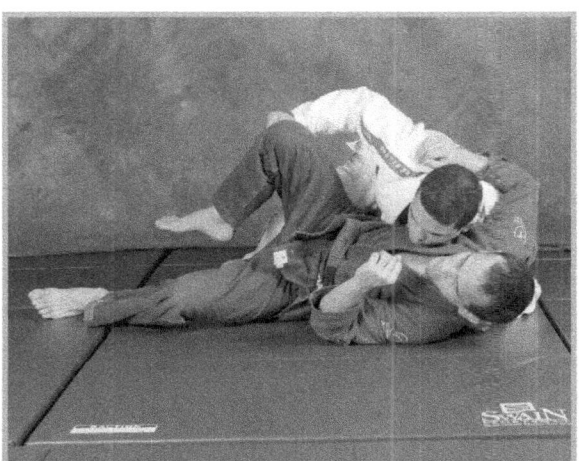

15. Gerson moves to the side, controlling the opponent's right leg with his right hand,

16. and applies a side control to initiate the offensive.

TECHNIQUE 6

THE OPEN GUARD

1. Gerson faces his opponent from an open guard.

2. The opponent moves his right knee to prepare to pass the guard. Gerson slides his body to the side...

3. and grabs the opponent's right sleeve with both hands.

4. Then, he brings his left leg to the outside...

5. to get momentum...

6. to bring it under the opponent's right leg as he simultaneously sits on the ground.

7. Gerson brings his right leg down and tries to grab the opponent's left sleeve,

8. but the opponent pulls his left arm and prevents Gerson from grabbing it.

(CONTINUED ON NEXT PAGE)

TECHNIQUE 6 (CONTINUED)

THE OPEN GUARD

(CONTINUED FROM PREVIOUS PAGE)

9. Gerson then brings his right hand and grabs the opponent's gi behind the neck.

10. He pulls him down…

11. and uses the hook of the left leg…

12. to sweep the opponent toward his right side.

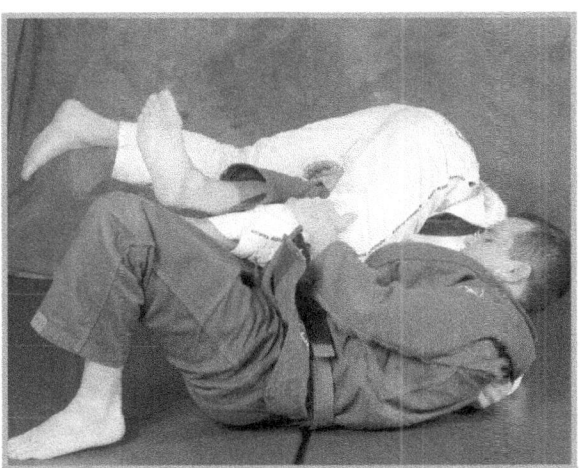

13. Gerson maintains control of the opponent's right leg through the action…

14. and ends up on the opponent's half guard…

15. that he passes to adopt the mount position to initiate the attack.

TECHNIQUE 7
THE OPEN GUARD

1. Gerson faces his opponent from an open guard.

2. The opponent moves his right knee, preparing to pass the guard.

3. Gerson slides his body to the side and grabs the opponent's right sleeve with both hands…

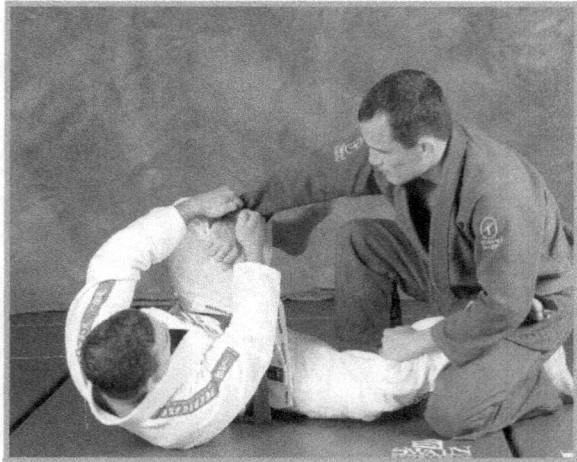
4. and pulls hard to break the opponent's grip.

5. Then, he starts to bring his left leg to the outside...

6. to get momentum...

7. to pass it under the opponent's right leg and place it on the opponent's stomach as he simultaneously slides his body to the side and maintains control of the opponent's right sleeve.

8. Gerson begins to apply more pressure on the opponent's stomach as...

(CONTINUED ON NEXT PAGE)

TECHNIQUE 7 (CONTINUED)

THE OPEN GUARD
(CONTINUED FROM PREVIOUS PAGE)

9. he pulls hard on the opponent's right sleeve.

10. He rolls with the opponent as he applies a sweep…

11. that makes the opponent land on his left side.

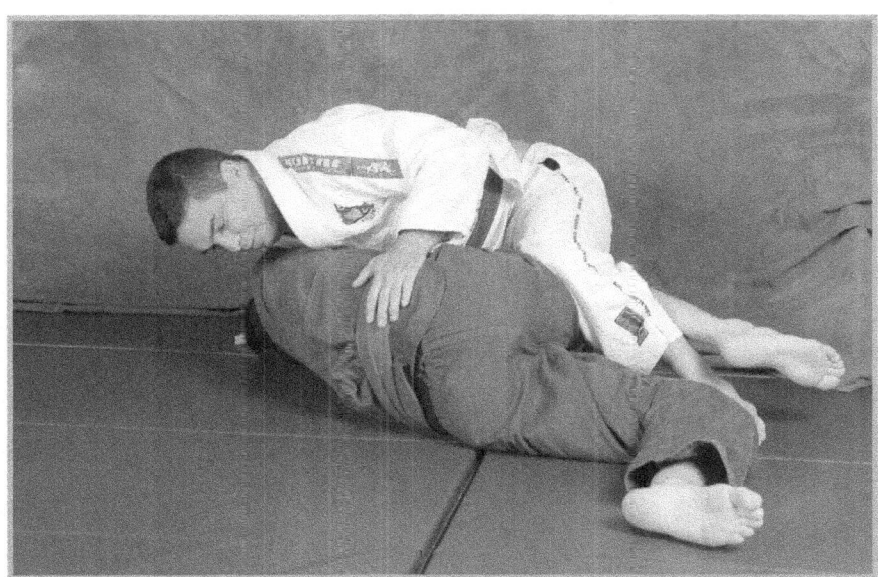

12. Gerson controls the opponent from the side...

13. and mounts him to get a full control before initiating the attack.

TECHNIQUE 8

THE OPEN GUARD

1. Gerson, on his back, faces the opponent standing and ready to pass the guard.

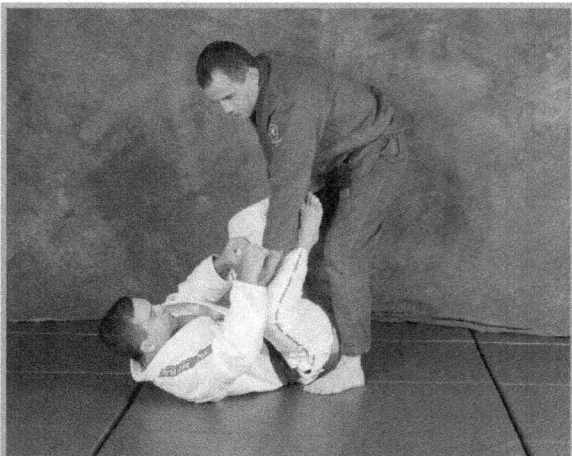

2. Gerson reaches out, grabs the opponent's left sleeve…

3. and pulls hard…

4. to break the grip on his right leg.

5. Then, he maintains control of the opponent's right sleeve with his left hand and brings his right leg behind the opponent's right knee in a hooking position.

6. Gerson uses his left foot, placed on the opponent's right hip, to slightly push away...

7. to create a little space...

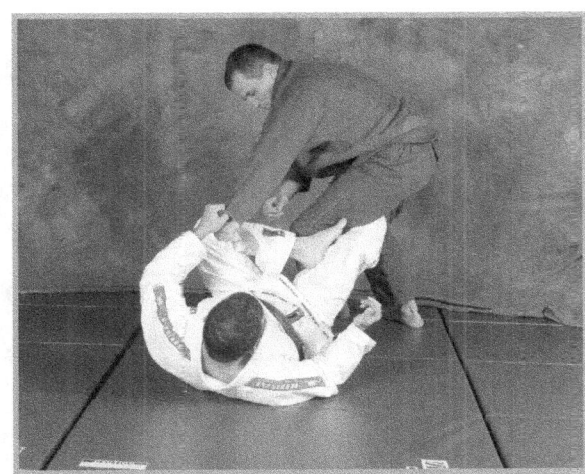

8. so he can now bring his left foot close to the right leg and,

(CONTINUED ON NEXT PAGE)

TECHNIQUE 8 (CONTINUED)

THE OPEN GUARD
(CONTINUED FROM PREVIOUS PAGE)

9. reversing the hooks, grab the opponent's belt from behind.

10. Then, he puts pressure on the hooks, pulls from the belt, and pulls on the opponent's left sleeve...

11. to bring the opponent right inside of his guard.

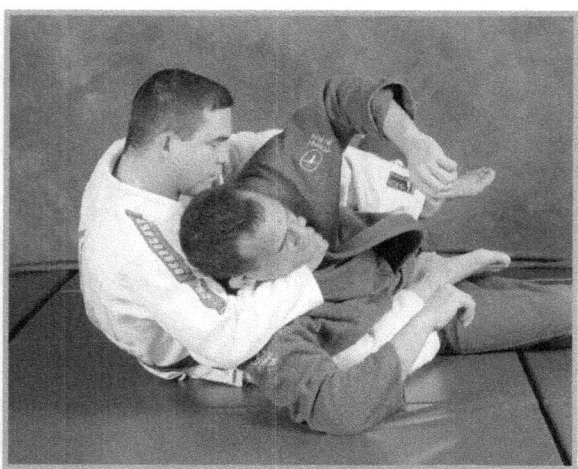

12. Gerson initiates the offensive by reaching the left side of the opponent's collar with his right hand,

13. and then the right side of the collar with the left hand.

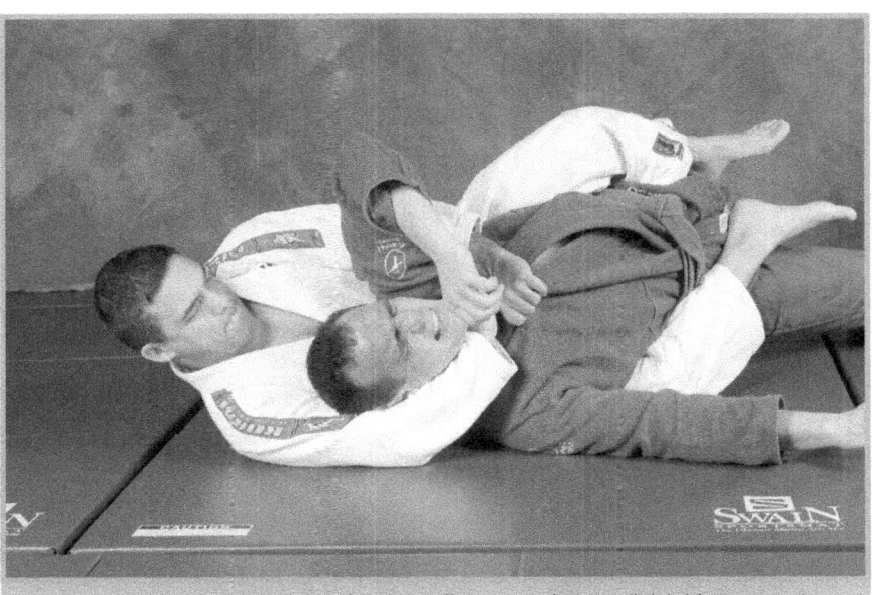

14. Finally, he pulls with both hands and applies a rear choke to finish his opponent.

TECHNIQUE 9
THE OPEN GUARD

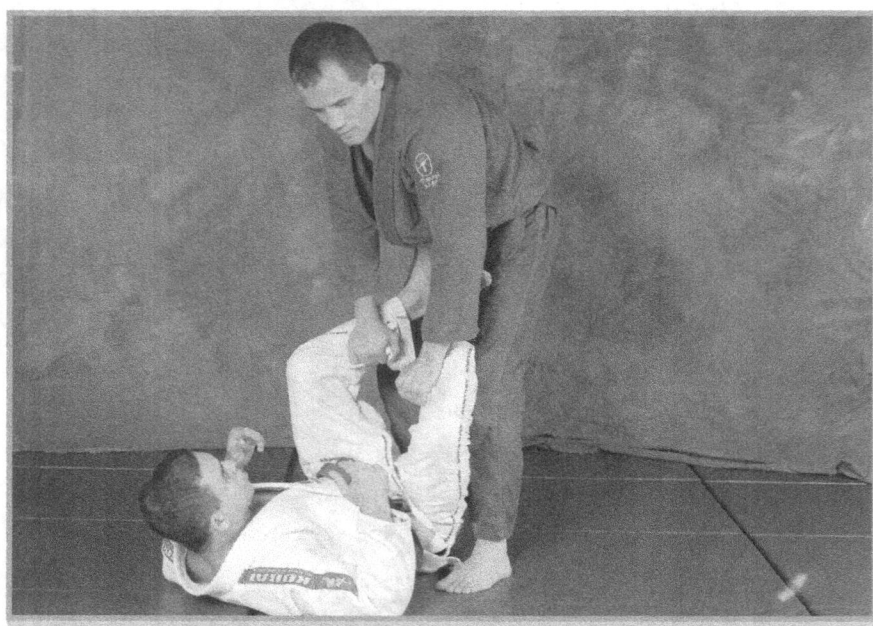

1. Gerson, on his back, faces the opponent standing and ready to pass the guard.

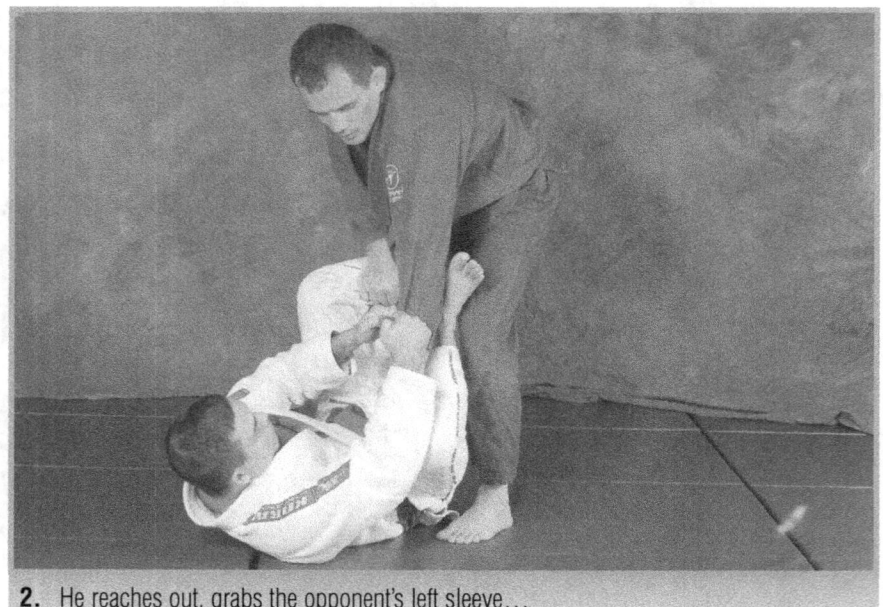

2. He reaches out, grabs the opponent's left sleeve...

3. and pulls hard to break the grip on his right leg.

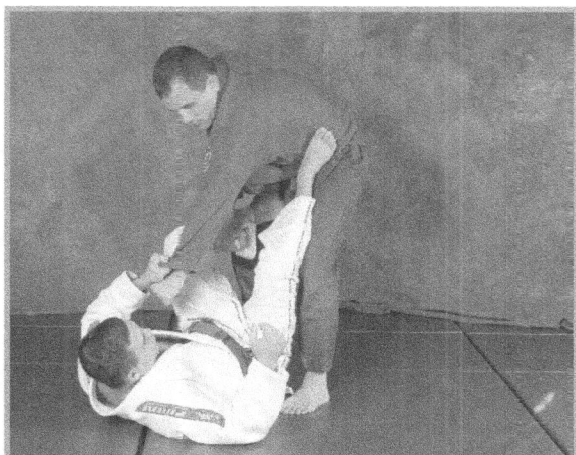
4. Then, he maintains control of the opponent's left sleeve with his left hand and brings his right leg to the opponent's left hip.

5. Now, with his right hand Gerson grabs the back of the opponent's left ankle...

(CONTINUED ON NEXT PAGE)

TECHNIQUE 9 (CONTINUED)

THE OPEN GUARD

(CONTINUED FROM PREVIOUS PAGE)

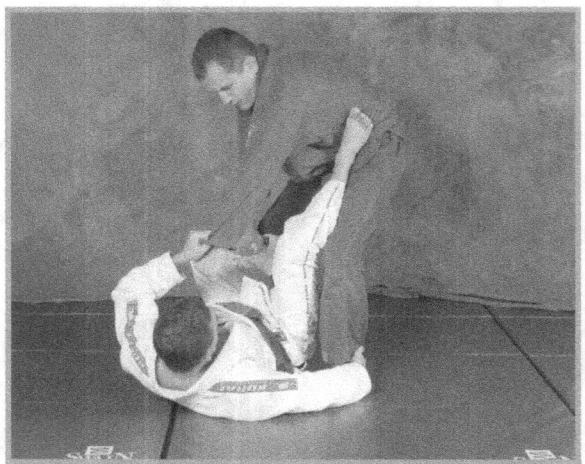

6. as he simultaneously uses his left foot as a hook behind the opponent's right leg.

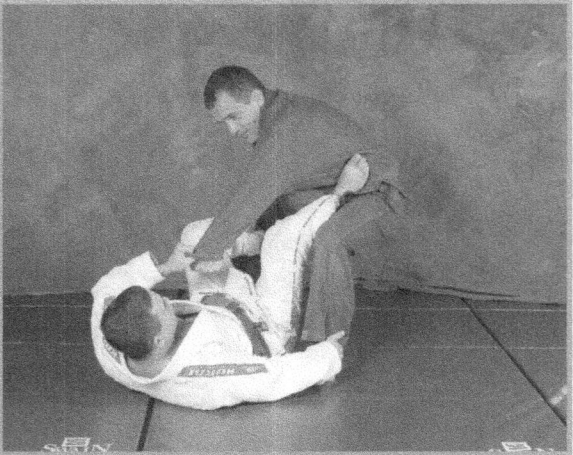

7. Then, he pulls with his right hand and, at the same time, pushes away with his right foot,

8. which sweeps the opponent onto the ground.

9. Gerson gets up with full control of the opponent's left arm,

10. and positions himself inside the opponent's guard to initiate the offensive.

TECHNIQUE 10
THE OPEN GUARD

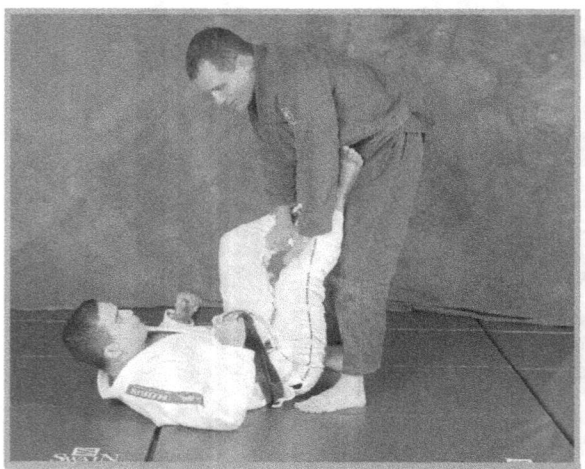

1. Gerson, on his back, faces the opponent standing and ready to pass the guard.

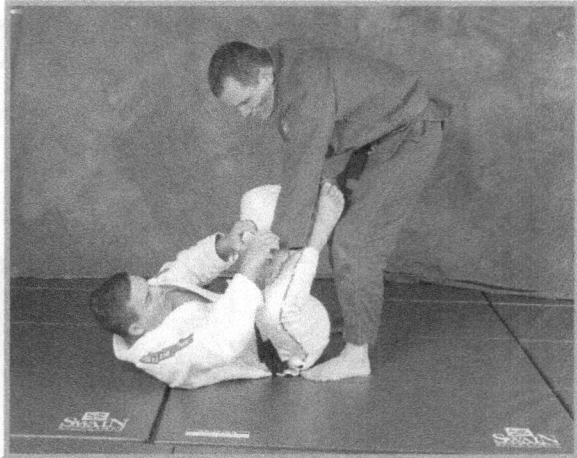

2. He reaches out,

3. grabs the opponent's left sleeve...

4. and pulls hard to break the grip on his right leg.

5. Then, he maintains control of the opponent's left sleeve with his left hand and brings his right leg to the opponent's left hip.

6. With his right hand, Gerson grabs the back of the opponent's left ankle…

7. and begins to pull with his right hand and to push the opponent's left hip away with his right foot.

(CONTINUED ON NEXT PAGE)

TECHNIQUE 10 (CONTINUED)

THE OPEN GUARD

(CONTINUED FROM PREVIOUS PAGE)

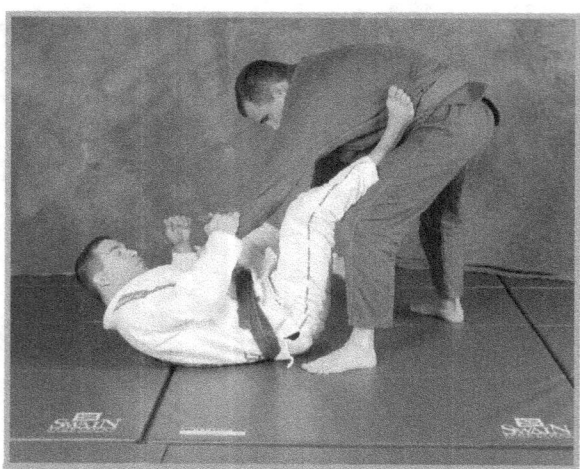

8. Gerson begins to rotate his body to the left...

9. and brings his left leg under the opponent's legs...

10. as he starts to push away with his right foot..

11. Then, he sweeps the opponent's left leg with his left foot, pushes hard with the right foot, and pulls the opponent's left sleeve with his right hand.

12. The opponent falls on the ground...

13. and Gerson continues his action...

14. by putting pressure and taking control on the half guard before initiating the offensive.

TECHNIQUE 11
THE OPEN GUARD

1. Gerson faces his opponent using the open guard, with both feet on the opponent's hips.

2. He slides his hips to the left side to create space to bring his right leg inside...

3. and puts his shin on the opponent's stomach.

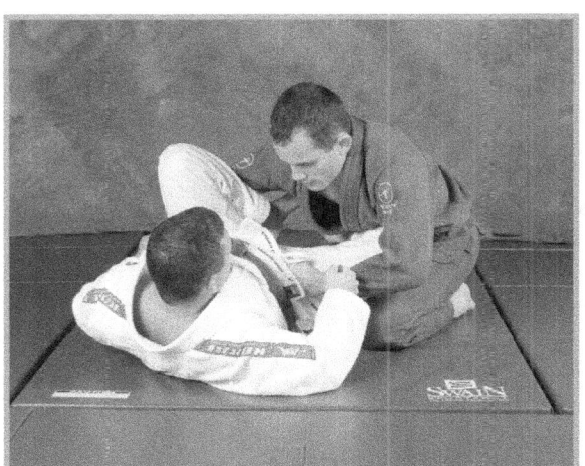

4. Then, he pulls the opponent's left sleeve to bring the body closer and on top of his right leg.

5. Gerson now grabs the opponent's pants at the knee level…

6. and begins to push to the left with his left thigh…

(CONTINUED ON NEXT PAGE)

TECHNIQUE 11 (CONTINUED)

THE OPEN GUARD

(CONTINUED FROM PREVIOUS PAGE)

7. as he simultaneously pushes with his right hand...

8. and sweeps the opponent by using his right shin.

9. Gerson follows the movement and puts pressure on the opponent's stomach with his right leg…

10. without releasing the grip on the opponent's right sleeve with his left hand.

TECHNIQUE 12

THE OPEN GUARD

1. Gerson faces his opponent using the open guard, with both feet on the opponent's hips.

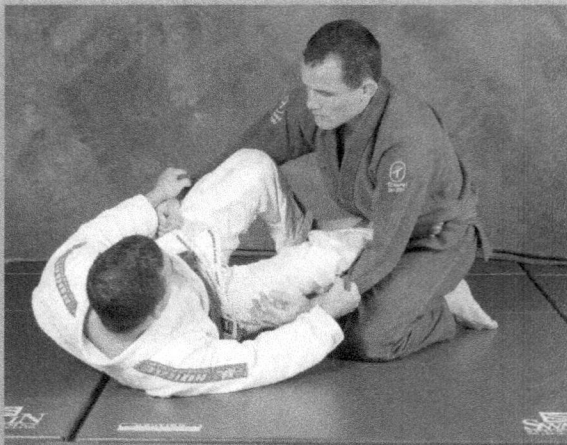

2. He slides his hips to the side...

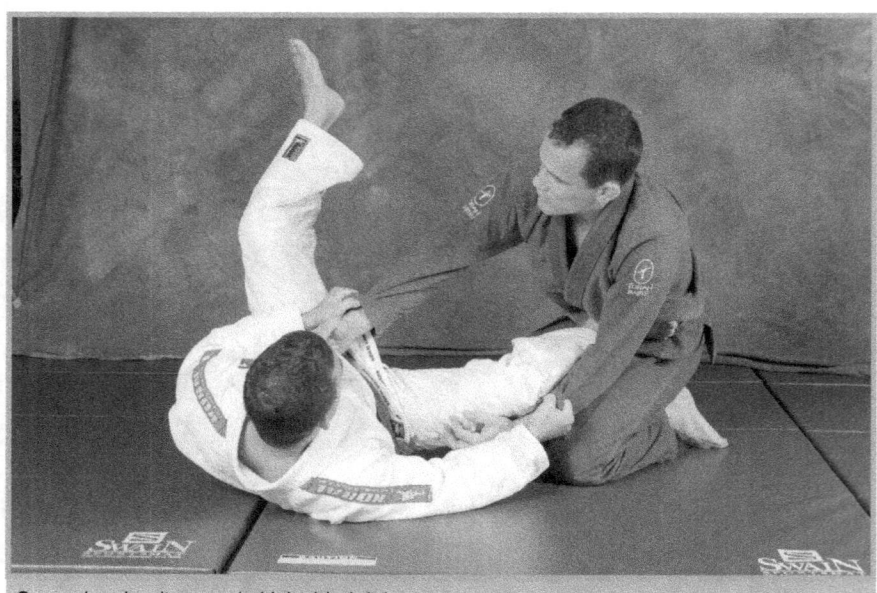

3. as he simultaneously kicks his left leg out...

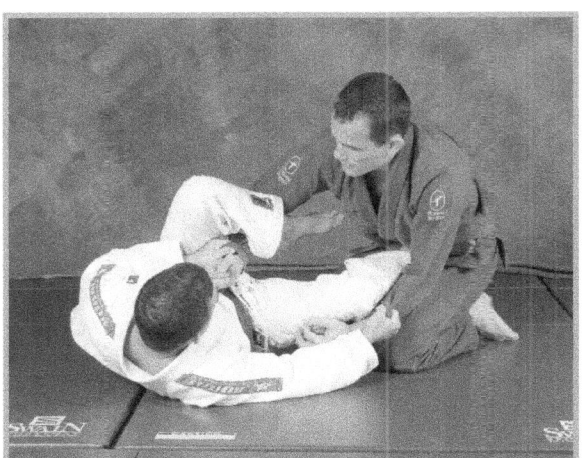

4. and brings it back, wrapping it around the opponent's right arm.

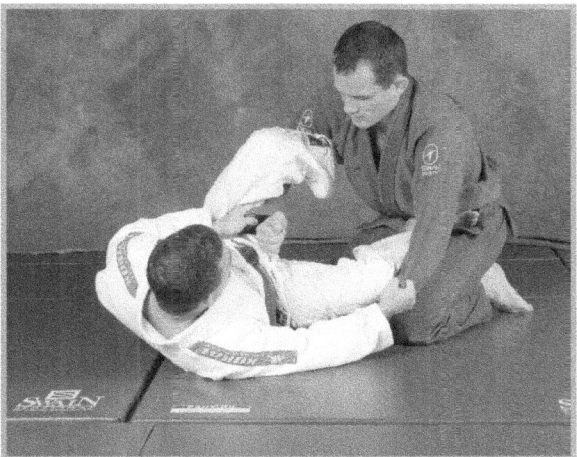

5. Then, Gerson puts his left foot under the opponent's armpit for a more secure positioning of the leg.

6. He pulls the opponent's left sleeve with his right hand…

(CONTINUED ON NEXT PAGE)

TECHNIQUE 12 (CONTINUED)

THE OPEN GUARD
(CONTINUED FROM PREVIOUS PAGE)

7. to bring the opponent's body closer.

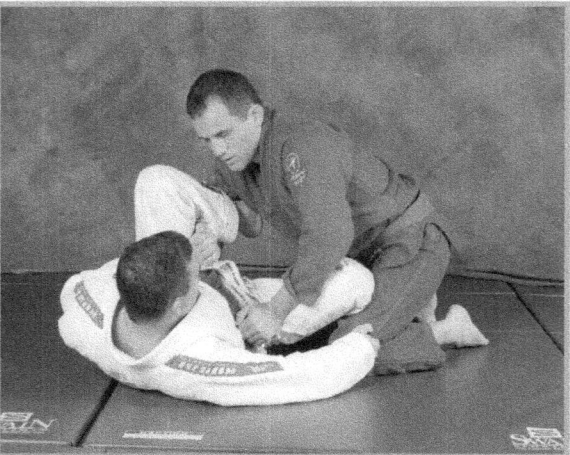

8. Then, he grabs the opponent's pants at the level of the left knee...

9. and pulls to bring him close to his own body for better leverage.

10. From here, Gerson pushes with his left leg and right hand as he simultaneously supports the movement with his right leg, which is under the opponent's stomach.

11. Once the opponent is on the ground,

12. Gerson takes full control of the action from a mounted position.

TECHNIQUE 13

THE OPEN GUARD

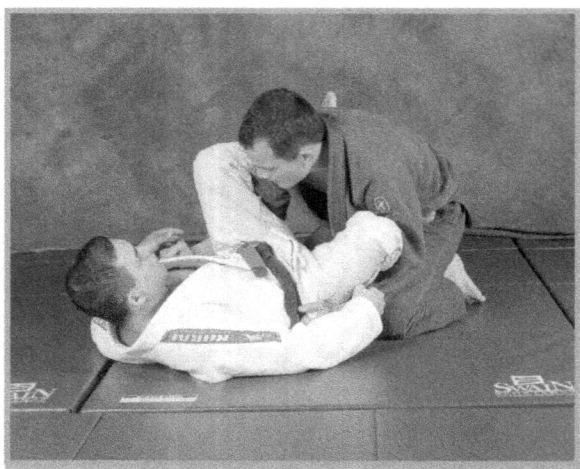

1. Gerson has the opponent inside the open guard, but this time his left leg is outside and over the opponent's right shoulder.

2. He starts to move the hips back a little bit...

3. and creates space sliding to the right side.

4. Then, he grabs the opponent's pant at the knee level of the left leg.

5. With his left hand, Gerson begins to pull the opponent's right hand as he simultaneously secures his right shin close to the opponent's stomach.

6. By using his left leg, he pushes the opponent's right arm to the side with his left leg and, at the same time, lifts the opponent's left leg with his right hand.

7. Once he has swept the opponent, Gerson maintains the control of the body,

8. and mounts his opponent with the right knee on the stomach to initiate the offensive.

THE OPEN GUARD

TECHNIQUE 14

THE OPEN GUARD

1. Gerson faces his opponent from an open guard.

2. The opponent moves his right knee to prepare to pass the guard. Gerson slides his body to the side and brings his left leg back.

3. Now he grabs the opponent's right sleeve with both hands...

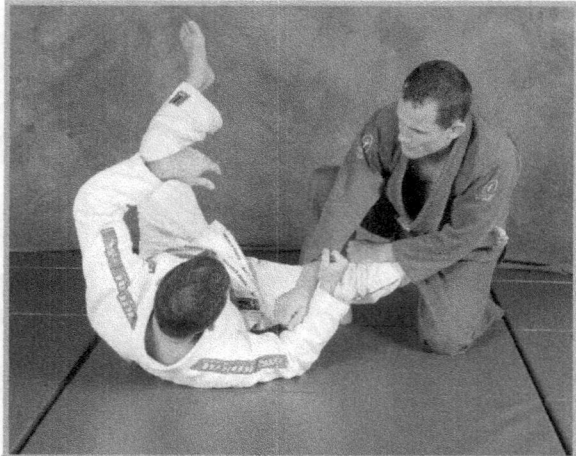

4. and he brings his left leg to the outside...

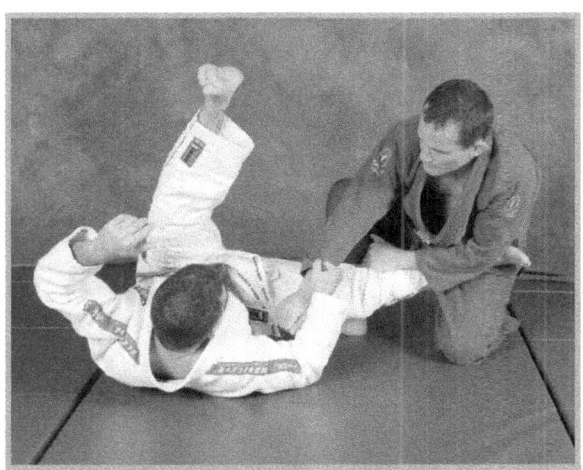

5. to get momentum...

6. to bring it under the opponent's right leg as he simultaneously sits on the ground.

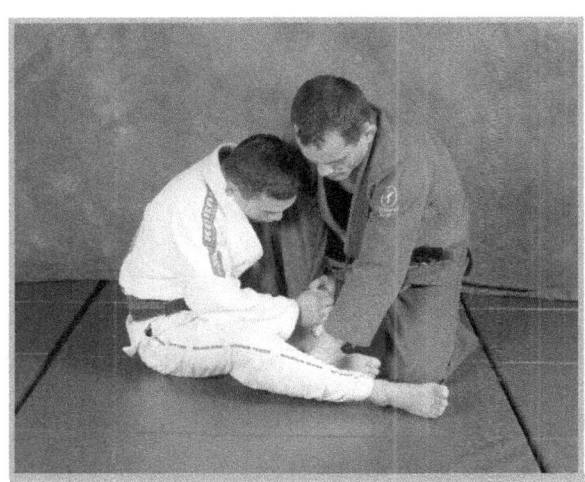

7. Gerson brings his right leg down and as he tries to grab the opponent's right sleeve with his right hand,

8. but the opponent stands up to avoid losing control.

(CONTINUED ON NEXT PAGE)

TECHNIQUE 14 (CONTINUED)

THE OPEN GUARD

(CONTINUED FROM PREVIOUS PAGE)

9. Gerson then moves to the side...

10. and slides under the opponent's body to grab the opponent's left leg.

11. He keeps circling in the same direction...

12. and sweeps the opponent...

13. onto the ground...

14. and on his back.

15. Gerson keeps control of the sweeps by holding to the opponent's left leg.

16. Then, he passes to the side control from where he will initiate the offensive.

THE OPEN GUARD

TECHNIQUE 15

THE OPEN GUARD

1. Gerson faces his opponent using an open guard with a double sleeve grip.

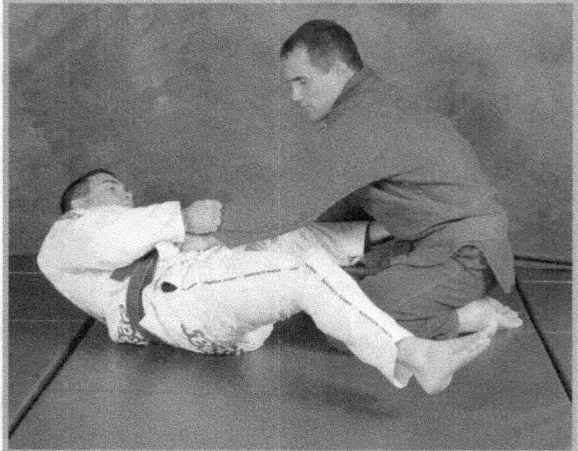

2. He moves his right leg to the side but maintains control of the opponent's body with his left foot on the opponent's right hip.

3. He brings the right leg over the opponent's left arm...

4. and hooks it tight under the opponent's right armpit.

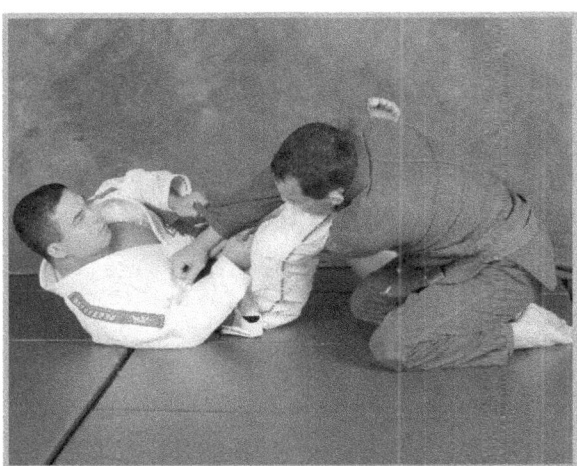

5. Gerson pulls hard with both hands of the opponent's sleeves…

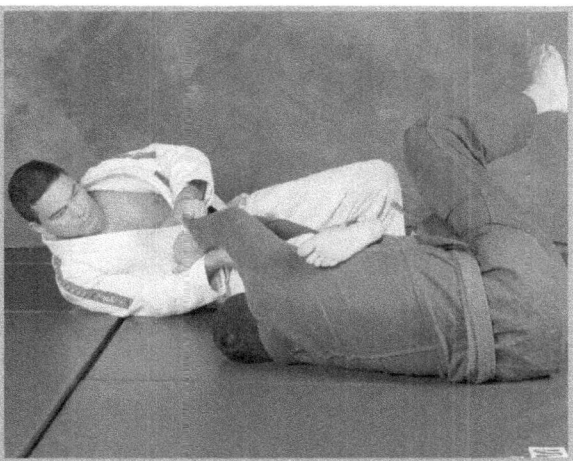

6. and simultaneously sweeps to the right with his right shin…

7. to bring the opponent to the ground.

8. Then, he applies a side control from where he will start his attack.

TECHNIQUE 16

THE OPEN GUARD

1. Gerson faces his opponent using an open guard with a double outside sleeve grip.

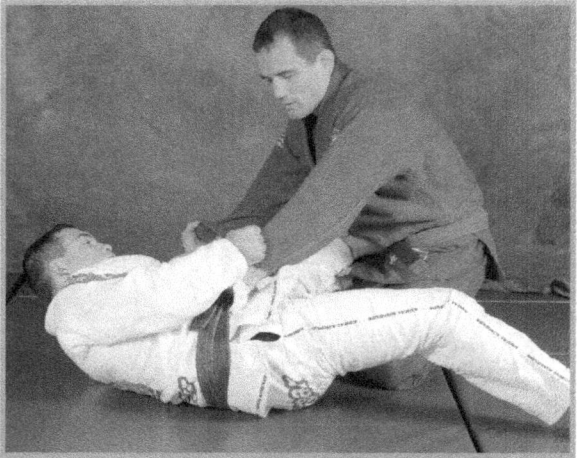

2. He moves his right leg to the side but maintains control of the opponent's body with his left foot on the opponent's right hip.

3. He brings the right leg over the opponent's left arm...

4. and hooks it tight under the opponent's right armpit.

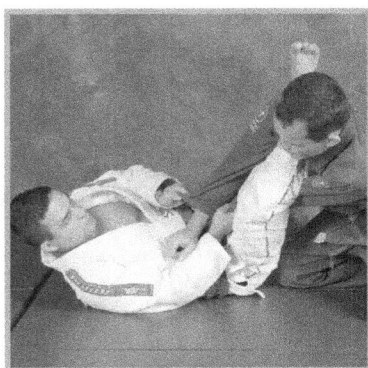

5. Gerson pulls hard with both hands of the opponent's sleeves...

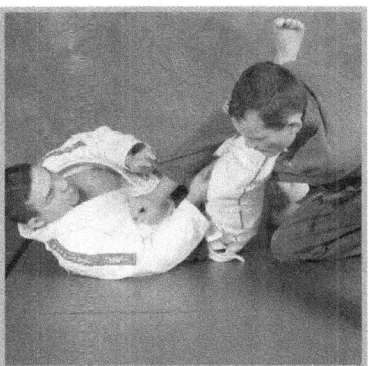

6. and simultaneously sweeps to the right with his right shin, to bring the opponent to the ground.

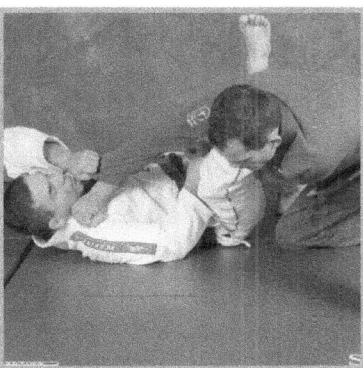

7. The opponent resists the sweeps and pushes away with his right arm.

8. Gerson see the impossibility of applying the sweep and changes his hip position to pass his left leg in front of the opponent's neck,

9. to apply a straight armlock from the guard.

TECHNIQUE 17
THE OPEN GUARD

1. Gerson faces his opponent using the open guard.

2. The opponent initiates his attack by using his right hand to pass the left side of Gerson's guard.

3. Merson slightly moves his hips to the left,

4. to create space as he begins to move his left leg...

5. across the opponent's face.

6. Then, he takes control of the opponent's right arm...

7. and grabs the opponent's pant at the knee level of the left leg.

8. Gerson begins to push away with his left leg and pull upward with his right hand as he simultaneously secures the opponent's right arm with his left hand.

(CONTINUED ON NEXT PAGE)

TECHNIQUE 17 (CONTINUED)

THE OPEN GUARD

(CONTINUED FROM PREVIOUS PAGE)

9. The opponent is swept,

10. and Gerson maintains full control of the action

11. He moves up and places his right knee on the opponent's stomach…

12. for a full side control from where he will initiate the offensive.

TECHNIQUE 18

THE OPEN GUARD

1. Gerson, on his back, faces the opponent standing and ready to pass the guard.

2. Gerson reaches out, grabs the opponent's left sleeve...

3. and pulls hard to break the grip on his right leg as he simultaneously kicks his right leg out,

4. so he can bring it inside the opponent's left leg.

5. Then he puts pressure with his right leg,

6. and grabs the opponent's left ankle with his right hand.

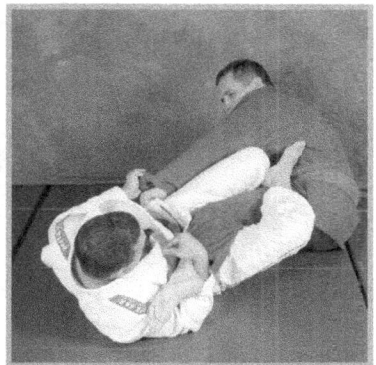

7. By pulling with his left hand and pushing with his left leg [on the opponent's right hip],

8. Gerson sweeps the opponent to the ground.

9. Then, he passes the opponent's left leg to the left side of his body and applies a painful knee-bar submission.

TECHNIQUE 19

THE OPEN GUARD

1. Gerson, using the open guard, faces his opponent.

2. The opponent pushes forward and Gerson moves his hips slightly back,

3. to immediately slide in back, adopting a seated position.

4. Then, he reaches out with his left hand and passes it around the opponent's left side of the body until he grabs the belt in the back.

5. Now, Gerson, with his right hand, grabs the opponent's left leg,

6. and using both feet as hooks, he pulls the opponent toward himself in a sweeps attempt.

(CONTINUED ON NEXT PAGE)

TECHNIQUE 19 (CONTINUED)

THE OPEN GUARD

(CONTINUED FROM PREVIOUS PAGE)

7. The opponent maintains a well-balanced position and it is impossible for Gerson to sweep him over.

8. Gerson immediately reassumes the front position, and taking advantage of the momentum created by the failed sweep attempt,

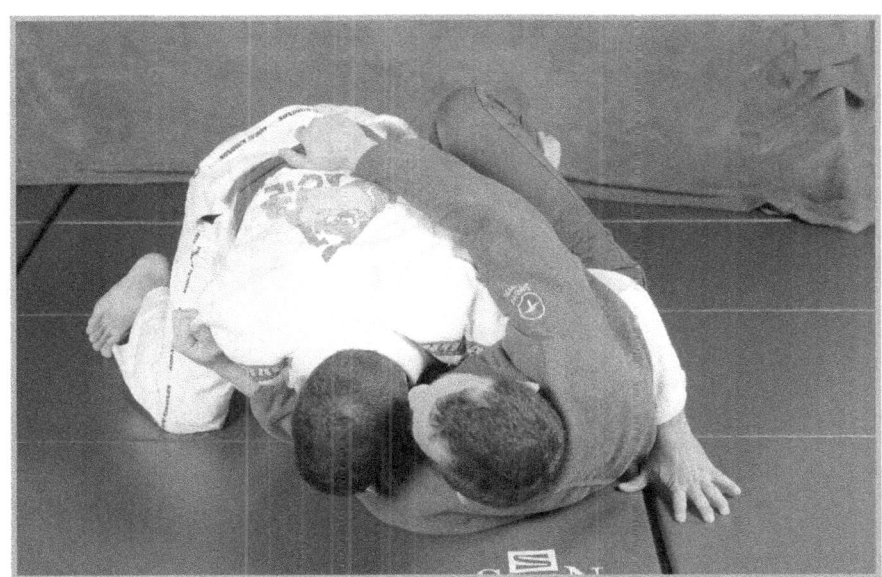

9. he pulls hard with his right hand and pushes around with his left to bring the opponent onto the ground.

10. Then, he adopts a full side control from where to initiate the attack.

TECHNIQUE 20

THE OPEN GUARD

1. The opponent is facing Gerson's open guard.

2. The opponent pushes forward but Gerson slightly moves his hips back,

3. to get momentum to lean forward and adopt a seated position...

4. from where he can come closer to the opponer's body and grab his left arm.

5. Then, he slides under the opponent's body...

6. and grabs the opponent's left leg under the knee.

(CONTINUED ON NEXT PAGE)

TECHNIQUE 20 (CONTINUED)

THE OPEN GUARD

(CONTINUED FROM PREVIOUS PAGE)

7. Gerson maintains a close position and, using his right hand grip on the opponent's left leg and the left hand securing the opponent's right side of the body,

8. he begins the sweep...

9. that throws the opponent to the left side.

10. Gerson maintains full control of the action...

11. and adopts a side control position...

12. from where he will initiate the offensive.

TECHNIQUE 21
THE OPEN GUARD

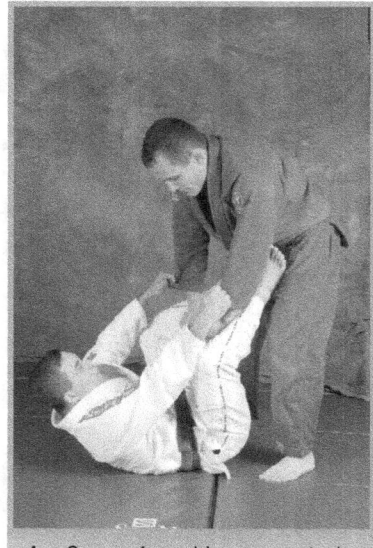

1. Gerson faces his opponent who has a tight grip on both of Gerson's pants.

2. Gerson kicks his left leg out as he simultaneously pulls hard from the opponent's right sleeve in order to break free from the opponent's control.

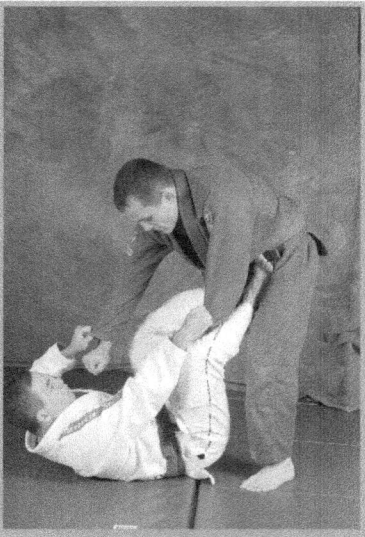

3. He brings his left leg under the opponent's right arm and places his left foot on the opponent's right hip,

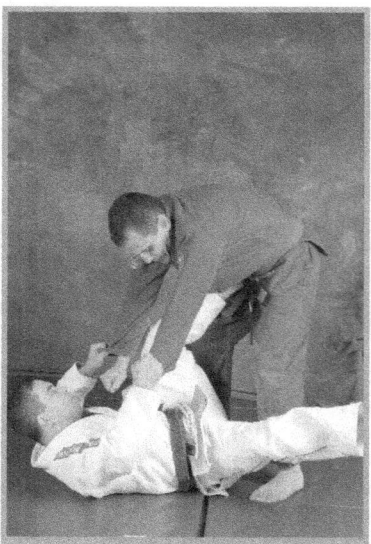

4. and does the same action with his right leg and right hand to break free on that side.

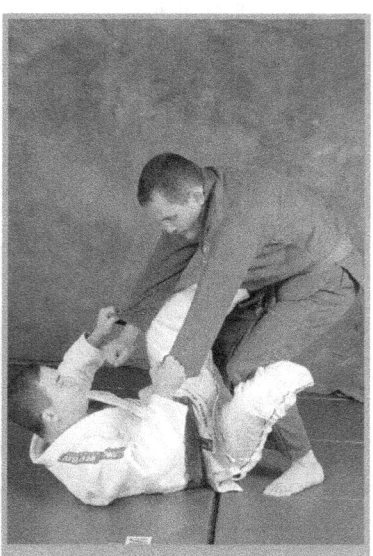

5. Then, he brings his right leg and wraps it around the opponent's left leg.

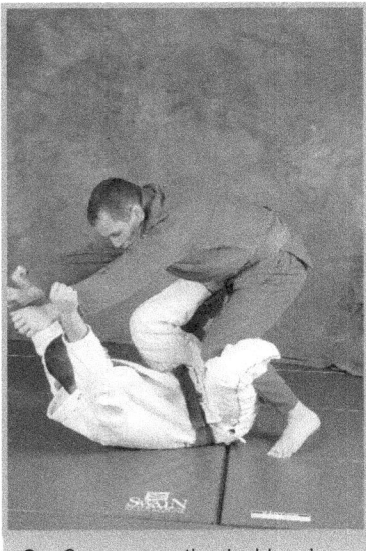
6. Gerson uses the double grip on the opponent's sleeves…

7. and pulls hard over his head…

8. as he simultaneously uses his right leg as a hook by bringing it closer,

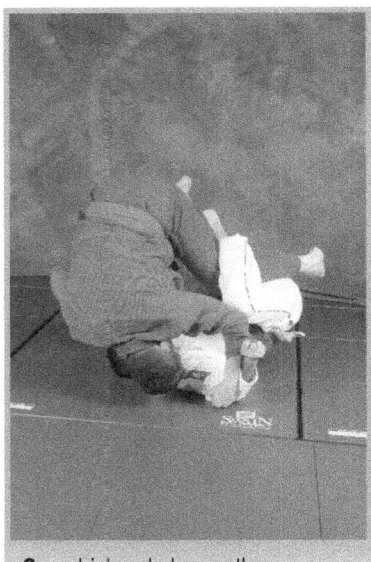
9. which unbalances the opponent,

10. and throws him over Gerson's body.

11. Gerson follows the rolling motion and ends on top of his opponent's chest.

TECHNIQUE 22

THE OPEN GUARD

1. Gerson has the opponent in the open guard.

2. Gerson's right hand has a tight grip on the right side of the opponent's collar.

3. He pulls hard with his left hand, which is grabbing the opponent's left sleeve, as he simultaneously brings the right leg…

4. to the outside and over the left side of the opponent's neck.

5. By using his left leg, Gerson keeps tight control of the opponent's body inside of his guard.

6. Then, he reaches with his left hand and grabs his own right ankle...

7. brings his right instep under the back of the left knee...

8. and secures the position.

9. Then, he passes the opponent's right arm to the right side of his body to have a better and tighter control and...

10. grabs the opponent's head with both hands pulling down to apply a triangle choke.

THE HALF GUARD

| Technique 1 . . . . . . 164 | Technique 3 . . . . . . 172 |
| Technique 2 . . . . . . 168 | Technique 4 . . . . . . 176 |

TECHNIQUE 1
THE HALF GUARD

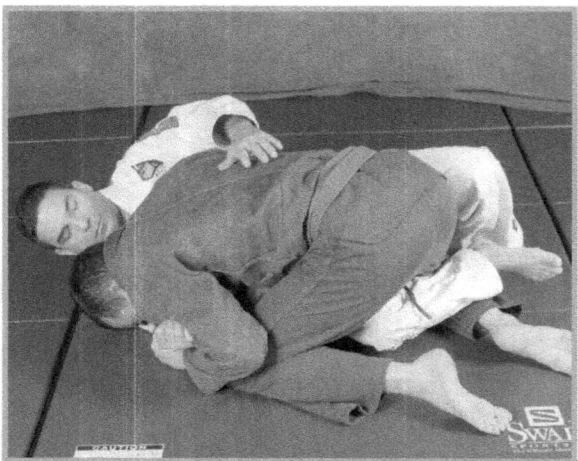

1. Gerson has his opponent on the right half-guard.

2. He slides his body backwards as he simultaneously pushes the opponent away...

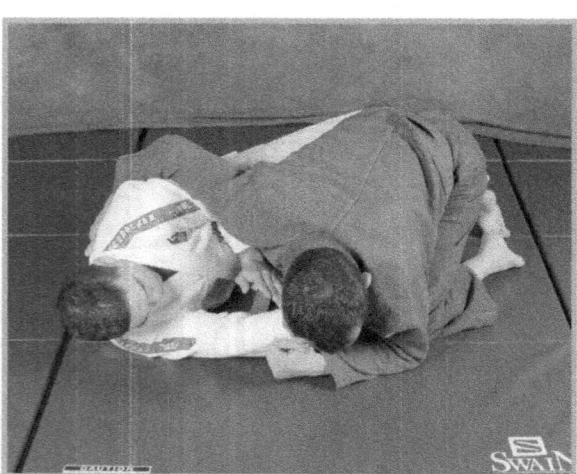

3. to create space so he can bring his left arm...

4. to the outside and over the opponent's back.

5. Then he brings the left arm to the side and, at the same time, slides his right leg out from between the opponent's.

6. Gerson secures his position and takes control of the opponent's body.

7. Then, he brings his left leg over and insert the hooks...

8. as he simultaneously pulls the opponent back.

(CONTINUED ON NEXT PAGE)

TECHNIQUE 1 (CONTINUED)

THE HALF GUARD

(CONTINUED FROM PREVIOUS PAGE)

9. The opponent tries to establish his position,

10. but Gerson brings him back...

11. and passes his right hand around his neck to reach for the left side of the opponent's collar.

12. Then, he secures his left hand grip over the right lapel of the opponent's gi,

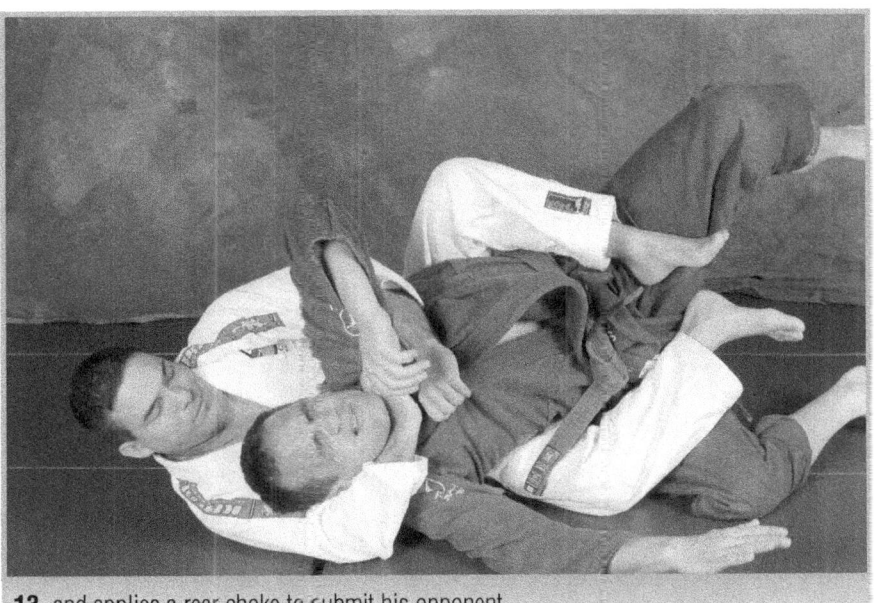
13. and applies a rear choke to submit his opponent.

TECHNIQUE 2
THE HALF GUARD

1. Gerson controls his opponent with a right half-guard.

2. He begins to slide his body toward the inside...

3. until he can reach the opponent's left ankle with his right hand.

4. Then, he moves his body backward and reaches the opponent's belt with his left hand to establish himself.

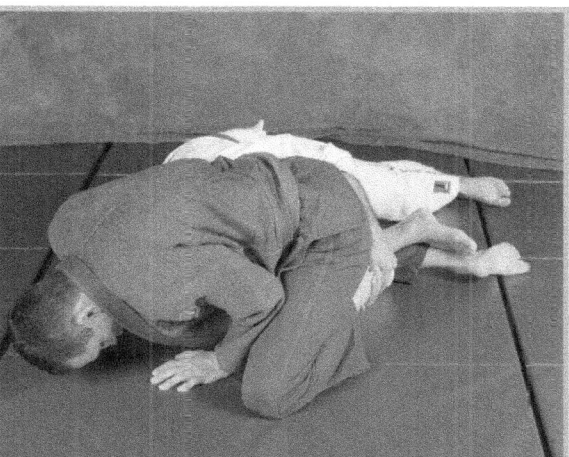
5. Immediately, he replaces the grip of his right hand with the left hand...

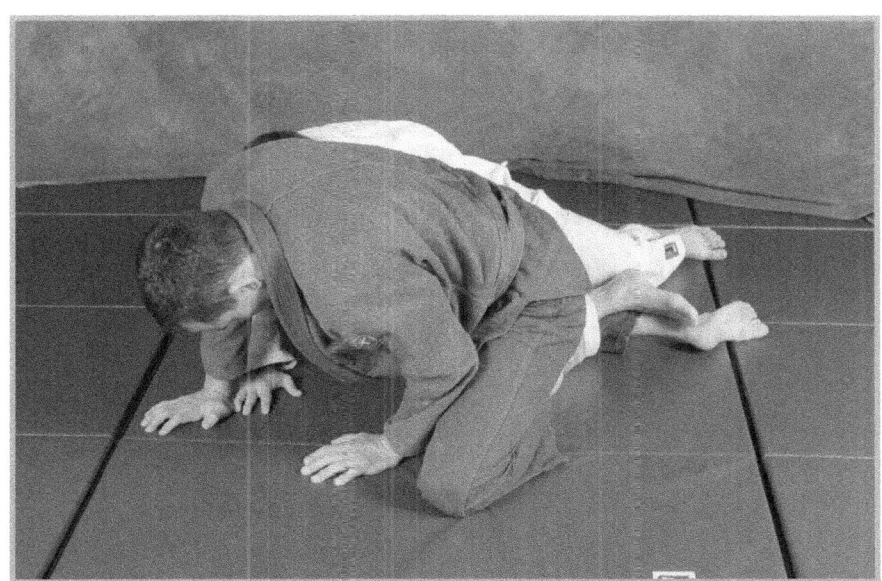
6. and uses his right hand to begin his escape action as the left hand grabs the opponent's ankle and secures it in place.

(CONTINUED ON NEXT PAGE)

TECHNIQUE 2 (CONTINUED)

THE HALF GUARD
(CONTINUED FROM PREVIOUS PAGE)

7. He moves his body out from under the opponent...

8. and reaches for the opponent's left leg.

9. Then, he pulls hard with both hands (ankle and leg)...

10. and rolls the opponent onto his back.

11. Then, Gerson applies a side control from where to take the initiative.

TECHNIQUE 3

THE HALF GUARD

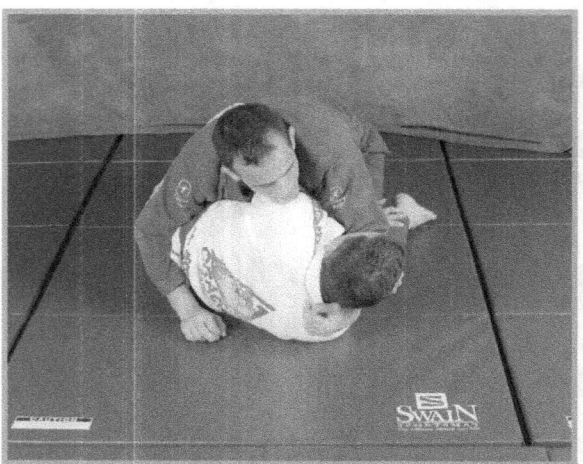

1. Gerson has the opponent on a right half-guard.

2. He moves to the right side and reaches for the opponent's leg.

3. He brings his right arm under the leg and grabs his own left hand.

4. Then, he secures the grip and pulls to the side to bring the opponent's leg to the front.

5. The opponent stops the action by sitting on Gerson's body.

6. Gerson reverse the grips and grabs the opponent's left sleeve…

7. as he simultaneously secures the opponent's right arm with his left hand.

8. Once he has a firm grip on both arms,

(CONTINUED ON NEXT PAGE)

TECHNIQUE (CONTINUED)

THE HALF GUARD
(CONTINUED FROM PREVIOUS PAGE)

9. he pulls hard to the side,

10. which brings the opponent out of balance,

11. rolling him to the left side,

12. from where Gerson can control the action...

13. by bringing his left arm under the opponent's head,

14. escaping his left leg,

15. and bringing his left knee close to the opponent's head…

16. for a final side control from where to initiate the offensive.

TECHNIQUE 4
THE HALF GUARD

1. Gerson has the opponent on a right half-guard.

2. He moves to the right side and reaches for the opponent's leg. He brings his right arm under the leg and grabs his own left hand.

3. Then, he secures the grip...

4. and pulls to the side to bring the opponent's leg to the front.

5. The opponent stops the action by trying to get up,

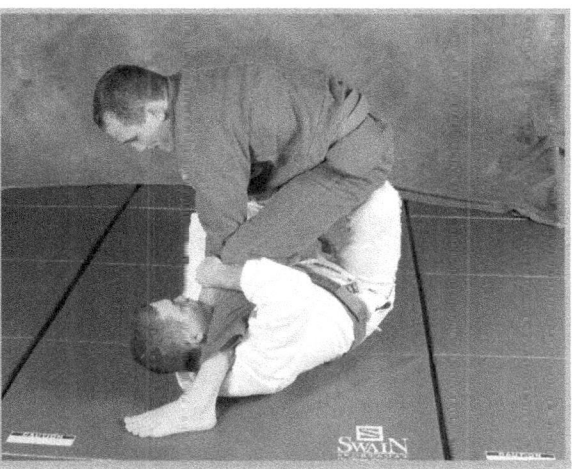
6. which blocks Gerson's action.

7. Gerson reverses the grips and grabs the opponent's left sleeve...

8. as he simultaneously secures the opponent's right arm with his left hand.

(CONTINUED ON NEXT PAGE)

TECHNIQUE 4 (CONTINUED)

THE HALF GUARD
(CONTINUED FROM PREVIOUS PAGE)

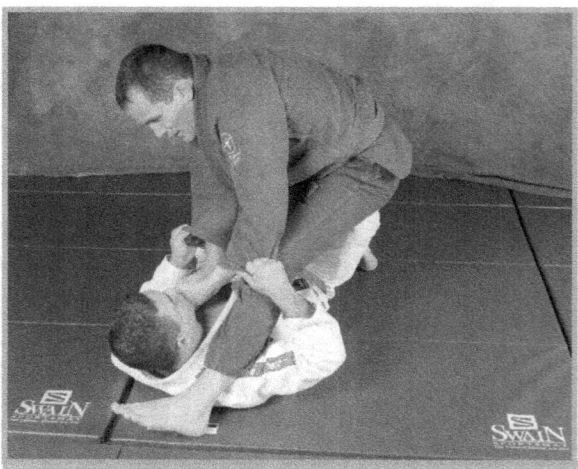

9. Once he has a firm grip on both arms,

10. he pushes backwards and...

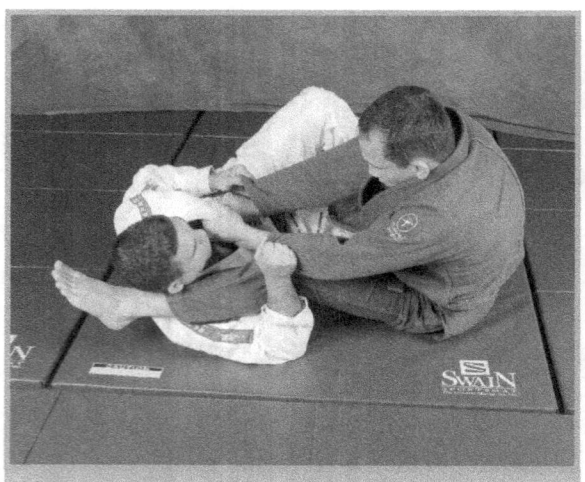

11. brings the opponent to the ground.

12. Gerson keeps the pressure and moves to the side...

13. so he can reach with his left hand...

14. and control the opponent's collar.

15. Once he has established the control, he moves his left arm around...

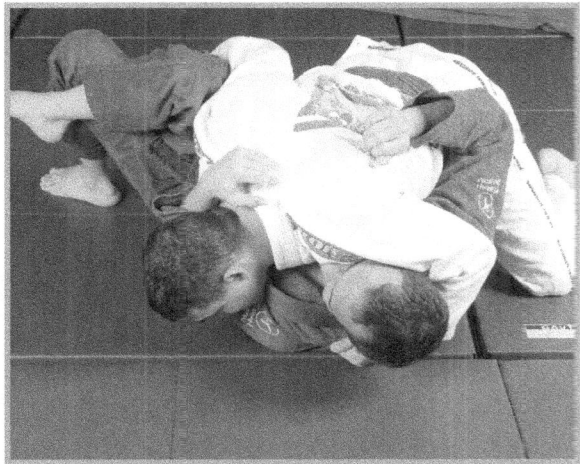

16. and adopts a perfect side control to initiate the offensive.

THE SPIDER GUARD

Technique 1 182	**Technique 3** 190
Technique 2 186	**Technique 4** 194

TECHNIQUE 1
THE SPIDER GUARD

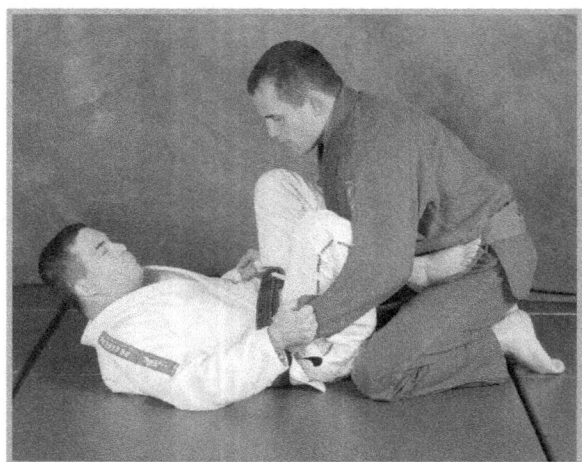

1. Gerson has his opponent in the open guard.

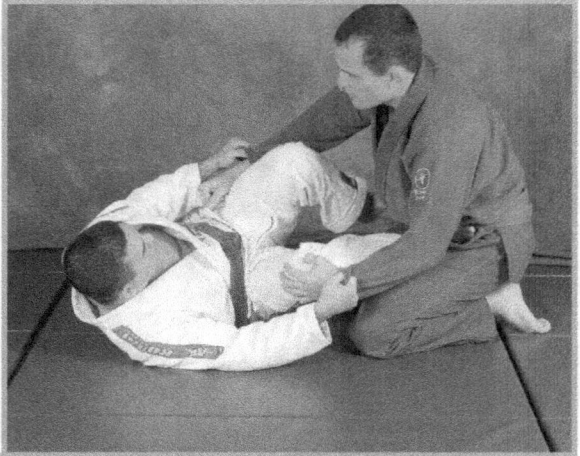

2. He moves his hips to the side...

3. and bring his left foot to the opponent's right biceps.

4. Then, he pulls hard on the opponent's left sleeve with his right hand...

5. and brings the right leg to the ground close to the opponent's left thigh.

6. Gerson pushes forward with his left leg, pulls with his right hand, and sweeps...

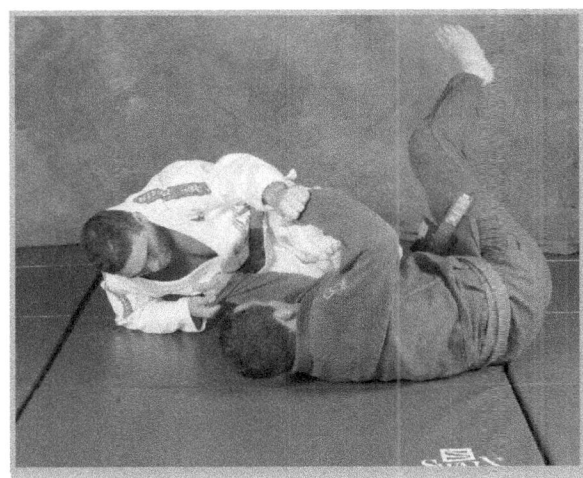

7. to the right with his right leg.

8. Immediately, he assumes the top position without releasing the grips...

(CONTINUED ON NEXT PAGE)

TECHNIQUE 1 (CONTINUED)
THE SPIDER GUARD
(CONTINUED FROM PREVIOUS PAGE)

9. and mounts the opponent as keeps the grip on the left hand.

10. He grabs the opponent's right wrist with his right hand,

11. brings his left arm under the opponent's right elbow,

12. and applies a bent-arm lock to finish his opponent.

TECHNIQUE 2
THE SPIDER GUARD

1. Gerson has his opponent in the open guard, securing both sleeves.

2. He slides his hips to the left side...

3. and bring his left foot to the opponent's right biceps.

4. Then, he pulls hard on the opponent's left sleeve with his right hand.

5. The opponent manages to put his left knee inside Gerson's right leg.

6. Gerson reacts by grabbing his pant at the knee level.

7. Then, he brings his opponent slightly forward...

8. and begins to sweep him to the left side

(CONTINUED ON NEXT PAGE)

TECHNIQUE 2 (CONTINUED)

THE SPIDER GUARD
(CONTINUED FROM PREVIOUS PAGE)

9. until the opponent's touches the ground.

10. Immediately, Gerson readjusts his position,

11. moves to the left side of his opponent as he maintains control of the opponent's right sleeve,

12. and assumes a perfect side control,

13. from where he can initiate the offensive.

THE SPIDER GUARD **189**

TECHNIQUE 3

THE SPIDER GUARD

1. Gerson has his opponent in the open guard, securing both sleeves.

2. He slides his hips to the left side,

3. and bring his left foot to the opponent's right bicep.

4. Then, he pushes with his left foot hard and pulls hard on the opponent's left sleeve with his right hand.

5. The opponent brings his left knee up to try to nullify Gerson's action.

6. Gerson moves slightly to the side and passes his right arm under the opponent's left leg.

7. Then, he turns his body…

8. and begins to push forward with the leg and arms…

(CONTINUED ON NEXT PAGE)

TECHNIQUE 3 (CONTINUED)

THE SPIDER GUARD

(CONTINUED FROM PREVIOUS PAGE)

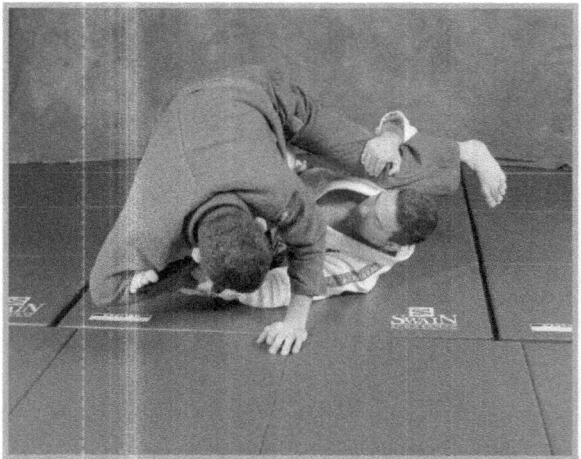

9. to bring the opponent out of balance and onto the ground.

10. Gerson, keeps the pressure by controlling the opponent's body during the fall.

11. Then, he adopts the side position,

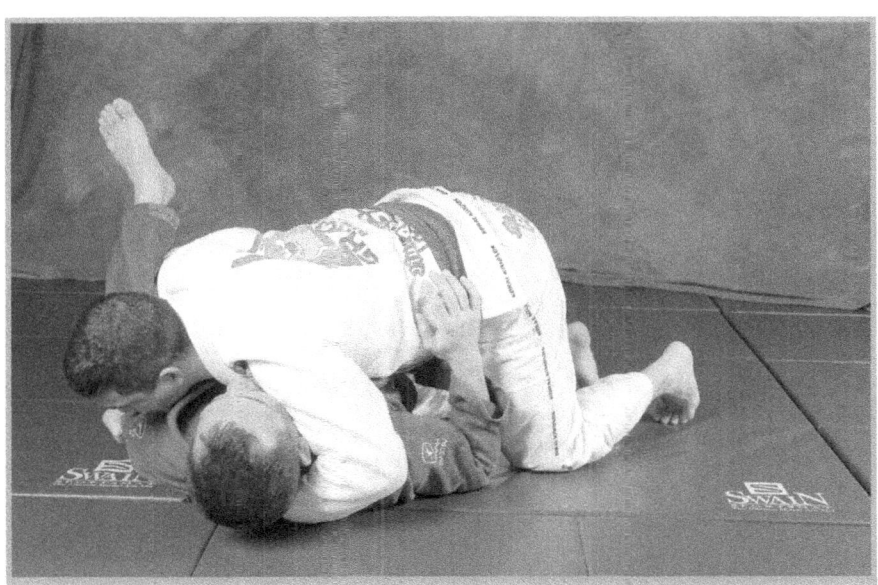

12. brings the knees all the way up and the left arm under the opponent's neck...

13. to fully control the situation and begin to take the offensive.

TECHNIQUE 4

THE SPIDER GUARD

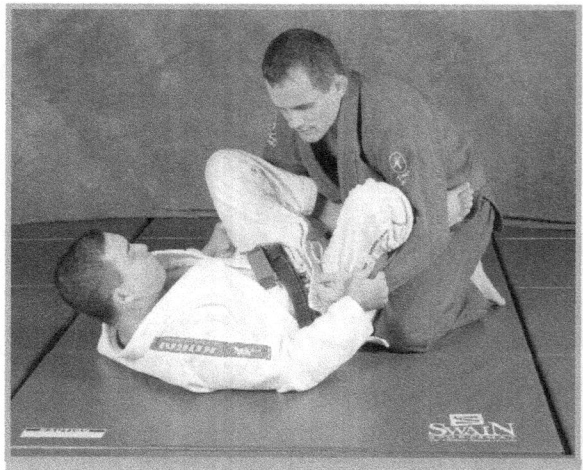

1. Gerson has his opponent in the open guard, securing both sleeves.

2. He slides his hips to the left side...

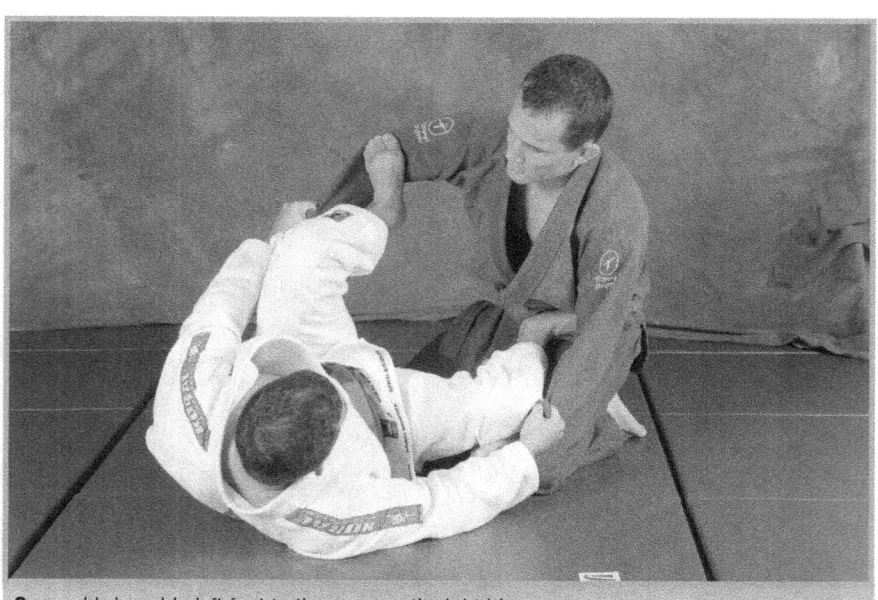

3. and brings his left foot to the opponent's right biceps.

4. Then, he pushes with his left foot hard and pulls hard on the opponent's left sleeve with his right hand,

5. which brings the opponent out of balance.

(CONTINUED ON NEXT PAGE)

TECHNIQUE 4 (CONTINUED)

THE SPIDER GUARD
(CONTINUED FROM PREVIOUS PAGE)

6. Gerson, brings the opponent's right arm behind his neck without releasing the grip...

7. and passes the left leg over the opponent's arm...

8. to secure the position of the leg over the opponent's neck as he simultaneously releases the grip from the sleeve and uses his right hand to better control the opponent's right arm.

9. With complete control of the body and the position, Gerson applies a final armlock.

EPILOGUE

You have finished this book. What have you learned?

Simply a series of practical and efficient techniques to become a successful Brazilian Jiu Jitsu practitioner. You have read about several methods and training practices that should help you be successful in competition and also grow from every defeat.

These techniques have been developed by world-class competitors who have successfully applied them in elite competition. These techniques have been shown to demonstrate that, through the same methods, you can obtain the same results as they did. But reading is not enough. Now, please go back and persistently practice each technique presented in these three volumes. Keep at it until you obtain the desired results.

We publish these books because of a sincere desire to help you. It will make us very happy if these volumes help you in your training. We have absolute confidence and belief in the principles and methods explained in this work. They have been tested in the "laboratory" of practical experience and real competition.

We may never meet in person, but in these books, we have met.

The Publishers

NOTES

NOTES

NOTES

www.ingramcontent.com/pod-product-compliance
Lightning Source LLC
Chambersburg PA
CBHW081347080526
44588CB00016B/2398